Praise for *Greek to Me*

"[Mary] Norris . . . whose first book chronicled her passion for punctuation, here recounts, with the same contagious wit and enthusiasm, her obsession with Greece—its language, history and culture."      —*New York Times Book Review*, Editors' Choice

"Beach reading for classicists and philhellenes . . . but with something more serious at stake." —A. E. Stallings, *Wall Street Journal*

"Norris is a jaunty companion, splendidly bookish, full of excellent little facts."      —Charlotte Higgins, *Guardian*

"Norris has a remarkable gift for conveying and transmitting passion." —Imogen Russell Williams, *Times Literary Supplement*

"Delightful."      —Bethanne Patrick, *Washington Post*

"*Greek to Me* bursts with a cheerful lust for all things Hellenic: the language, ancient and modern; the mythology; the wine; the sunshine; the sea; and, occasionally, the men."
—Susan Storer Clark, *Washington Independent Review of Books*

"Delightful and insightful."      —Nick Kampouris, *Greek Reporter*

"Written entertainingly, . . . *Greek to Me* is a travelogue, Mythology 101 course, lesson in linguistics and memoir on how a Catholic girl from Cleveland shed her timid skin and found meaning in another culture."      —David Luhrssen, *Shepherd Express*

"[Norris's] boundless curiosity and giddy enthusiasm will sweep you up and into her stories."　—Ilona Wallace, *Adelaide Review*

"Norris weaves her love of the Greek language into a brisk, witty book."　—Rob Thomas, *Capital Times* (Wisconsin)

"Captivating. . . . Norris' inviting book thrives on the writer's unabashed enthusiasm to learn, to immerse herself in the new and to find clues to her own past in the newly discovered."
—Robert Weibezahl, *BookPage*

"The book is a delicious intersection of personal essays, etymology, and travel writing. Norris' full Greek immersion pushed her out of her comfort zone and taught her much more than the history of the comma."　—*Booklist*

"Mary Norris's love for all things Greek is palpable and infectious. She is a charming, insightful guide through both ancient and modern glories, and I expect her lush descriptions of the Greek countryside to provoke a tourism stampede."　—Madeline Miller

"As a reader, I would follow the writer Mary Norris wherever she goes, and I found myself enthralled by this wondrous journey through Greek myths and language and art. Norris brings everything into the glimmering light—most of all the beauty of words."
—David Grann

"Poignant, antic, hilarious, Mary Norris is the definition of wearing your learning lightly, and after a lifetime of Greek immersion, pouring beer libations, and skinny-dipping in the waters of Aphrodite, her lessons slip down sweetly. This book is true ambrosia."

—Caroline Fraser

"Mary Norris, our master grammarian, proves that knowing the rules sets you free. Here she writes about Greek language, culture, and mythology with an untrammeled grace that's a delight to read and, almost incidentally, a demonstration of high-level literary skill. *Greek to Me* is a book to dive into—a page-turning and wonderful achievement."

—Ian Frazier

ALSO BY MARY NORRIS

*Between You & Me: Confessions of a Comma Queen*

# GREEK TO ME

Adventures of the Comma Queen

## MARY NORRIS

**W. W. NORTON & COMPANY**
*Independent Publishers Since 1923*

For information about permission to reproduce selections from this book,
write to Permissions, W. W. Norton & Company, Inc., 500 Fifth Avenue,
New York, NY 10110

For information about special discounts for bulk purchases, please contact
W. W. Norton Special Sales at specialsales@wwnorton.com or 800-233-4830

Manufacturing by LSC Communications, Harrisonburg
Book design by Ellen Cipriano
Production manager: Anna Oler

Library of Congress Cataloging-in-Publication Data

Names: Norris, Mary 1952– author.
Title: Greek to me : adventures of the comma queen / Mary Norris.
Description: First edition. | New York : W. W. Norton & Company, 2019.
Identifiers: LCCN 2018050108 | ISBN 9781324001270 (hardcover)
Subjects: LCSH: Norris, Mary 1952– —Travel—Greece. | Periodical
editors—United States—Biography. | Americans—Greece—Biography. |
Greece—Description and travel. | Greek language—Social aspects.
Classification: LCC PN4874.N638 A3 2019 | DDC 306.442/81—dc23
LC record available at https://lccn.loc.gov/2018050108

ISBN 978-0-393-35786-8 pbk.

W. W. Norton & Company, Inc., 500 Fifth Avenue, New York, N.Y. 10110
www.wwnorton.com

W. W. Norton & Company Ltd., 15 Carlisle Street, London W1D 3BS

1 2 3 4 5 6 7 8 9 0

*For Miles and Dee*
*and in memory of our parents,*
*Miles and Eileen Norris.*

It is ever to be borne in mind that though the outside of human life changes much, the inside changes little, and the lesson-book we cannot graduate from is human experience.

—EDITH HAMILTON,
*THE GREEK WAY*

# CONTENTS

# INVOCATION

SING IN ME, O Muse, of all things Greek that excite the imagination and delight the senses and magnify the lives of mortals, things that have survived three thousand years and more, since the time before the time of Homer, things that were old then and are new now—you know, the eternal. If that's not too much to ask, Muse. Please?

I don't know what gave me the idea I was good at foreign languages. I was an indifferent student of French in high school, though I longed to study at the Sorbonne instead of on the banks of the Cuyahoga. When I was in about fifth grade, my father refused to let me study Latin. The nuns had handpicked some students for a Saturday Latin class, and I was keen on it, but Dad flatly refused. My father was a pragmatic man. He worked for the fire department—one day on and two days off—and he could do anything around the house: roofing, plumbing,

1

carpentry, laying linoleum. He grew up during the Depression, when jobs were scarce, so for him security was paramount.

When I asked Dad to let me study Latin, he stamped out that flame like a pro in his fireman's boots. Was Dad against education for women? Yes. Was he worried I would come too much under the spell of the nuns and join the convent instead of getting married and settling down in the neighborhood? Probably. Had he missed the story of how the father of John Milton, recognizing the lad's genius, had him tutored in Latin and Greek from earliest youth? Apparently. Had he been scarred by a dead language? Yes! As a teenager, my father, who had been kicked out of three high schools, was sent by my grandmother to Ontario, Canada, to stay with his uncle, who had been educated as a Jesuit seminarian but backed out just before taking his final vows—went over the wall, as they say—and returned to Ontario to farm pigs. Uncle Jim taught my father a few things, and my father passed them on to us at the dinner table, such as the proper way to feed a horse an apple (with the palm flat) and the myth of Sisyphus, whose eternal punishment was to roll a boulder up a mountain and have it always roll back down, so he had to start over again. It sounded like a particularly bleak life lesson. What activity might merit a statuette in the shape of Sisyphus? Renewed effort in the face of certain failure? Undying hope? Persistence in ordinary life? Anyway, my father associated the classics with punishment, the eternal damnation of Sisyphus in Tartarus or the temporary banishment of a juvenile delinquent to the remote home of his maternal ancestors in rural Ontario. So when the nuns invited me to study Latin on Saturdays, Dad said, "No way," and I missed that first chance to learn Latin while my brain was at its most absorbent.

In college, I continued with French for a year and then dropped it. My junior year, I took a course in linguistics and had a flare-up of lust for Latin. I would soon graduate and have to decide what to do next, and I had just figured out that four years of a liberal-arts education was a delightful absurdity, a legitimate escape from real life, from Richard Nixon and the Vietnam War, a deferral of career and responsibility. I would study Latin, a dead language, for the sheer impracticality of it. I would know the joy of being a total nerd. But my linguistics professor, Whitney Bolton, talked me out of it. Latin, he said, would serve only to teach me about English. I didn't think to ask what was wrong with that. Remember, many linguists believe we are born hardwired to acquire language: I didn't need Latin to know English. Professor Bolton, whom I liked—he had a round head and a buzz cut, and reminded me of Anthony Hopkins as Richard the Lionheart in *The Lion in Winter*—told me I would be better off studying a living language, one that I could use in my travels. How did he know I wanted to travel? And Latin was spoken only in the Vatican. So I scratched that itch by taking a year of German. I've traveled a lot since then, but not in Germany, where Oktoberfest would no doubt have untied my tongue. Meanwhile, German did teach me a lot about English.

My taste for dead languages lay dormant until circa 1982 AD, at which point I had been working at *The New Yorker* for about four years, doing my best to master the Major Arcana of *New Yorker* style for a job on the copydesk. I had worked my way up to the collating department, where I basically got to see what everyone else did and study various editorial biases and skills. Collating, which has long since been replaced by the word processor, might be described as the liver of *The New Yorker*'s editorial process. Proofs arrived from a piece's editor, the author, the editor-in-chief (then William Shawn), Eleanor Gould (*The New Yorker*'s famous grammarian), proofreaders, fact checkers, and the libel lawyer, and we collators copied the changes the editor had accepted onto a clean proof for the printer, filtering out the dross, and sent the collated proof via fax (state of the art at the time) to the printer. Overnight, a revision appeared. The big excitement was being able to flag a mistake and save embarrassment. Once, coming back from lunch, I found the editor Gardner Botsford at my desk, taking refuge from a demanding author, who was just then on her way down the hall, calling, "Gardner?"

One weekend, I saw *Time Bandits* in a theater on the Upper East Side. In the film, directed by Terry Gilliam, of Monty Python's Flying Circus, and starring John Cleese and Michael Palin, a band of time-traveling dwarves plunder treasure from the past. One scene, set in ancient Greece, featured Sean Connery in a cameo as Agamemnon. He was dueling with a warrior who wore the head of a bull and looked like the Minotaur. The landscape was so stark and arid, and so enhanced by the mighty figure of Sean Connery in armor, that I wanted to go there right away. It didn't matter that the Minotaur was from Crete—his labyrinth was at Knossos, near Heraklion—and that Agamemnon was famously from the Peloponnese: he and his brother Menelaus were sons of Atreus, who was the son of Pelops, for whom the peninsula was named. The glory of Sean Connery blinded me to the screenwriters' twist on mythology. I was also unaware that the scenes set in Greece had been shot in Morocco.

The movie brought back to me some research I had done in grade school for a geography project. I was paired up with a boy named Tim, the class clown, and assigned a report on Greece. We (mostly I) made a poster that featured the main products of Greece, and I was impressed that a land so dry and stony—as in the movie, no grass, no green, more goats than cows—yielded olives and grapes, which could be pressed into oil and wine. It amazed me that such an austere land produced such luxuries.

The day after seeing *Time Bandits*, I told my boss at *The New Yorker*, Ed Stringham, that I wanted to go to Greece. Ed was the head of the collating department. He was famous at the office for his eccentric schedule and rigorous course of studies, and for his genius in suggesting books to people. He came in at about noon and held court from a tattered armchair by the window (kept firmly closed), smoking cigarettes and drinking takeout coffee. His friend Beata would come in—Beata had known W. H. Auden (she called him Wystan) and Benjamin Britten in Amityville. Alastair Reid, the Scottish poet and translator of Borges, would stop by to talk. Ed typically stayed at the office reading till one or two in the morning. My little brother, who was studying music, had a night job cleaning the floors in the business department and would come up and talk to Ed about Philip Glass and Gregorian chant.

When Ed heard that I wanted to go to Greece, he got all excited. There was a map of Europe on the wall, and he showed me where he had gone on his first trip to Greece. He'd taken a cruise, he said, apologetically, to get an overview: Athens, Piraeus, Crete, Santorini (or Thira, on the inner edge of a caldera that tourists rode up on donkeys), Rhodes, Istanbul. He went back many times: Thessaloniki and Meteora, to the north; Ioannina and Igoumenitsa, to the west, on the way to Corfu; and the Mani, the middle member of the three peninsulas that hang off the Peloponnese, where blood feuds raged between clans for generations. He pointed out Mount Athos, the Holy Mountain, a peninsula reserved for Orthodox monks, where no female, not even a hen, was welcome. Then he plucked a slim paperback off the shelf—*A Modern Greek Reader for Beginners*, by J. T. Pring—bent over it till his eyes were inches from the page, and started to translate.

"You can read that?" I said, astonished. It had never occurred to me that a person could become literate in a language that was written in a different alphabet.

"Of course," he replied, straightening up and refocusing his eyes, which were blue and wobbled in their sockets.

Seeing Ed unlock a Greek sentence gave me a Helen Keller moment: Greek could be lucid! It did not have to be unintelligible, as in the famous words of Casca in Shakespeare's *Julius Caesar*: "It was Greek to me." Those letters could be penetrated, and here was the proof. I had adored learning to read and write as a child, matching letters to sounds, building words, deciphering signs on restaurants and labels on cans of peas—cracking the code of literacy. After a steady diet of English and American literature through college and graduate school, I still relished the rules of phonics and enjoyed the nuts and bolts of syntax. And now I could get a fresh start with a whole new alphabet. I was incredibly excited. I was back in fifth grade again, and Dad had said yes!

BEFORE LONG, Ed had become my mentor in all things Greek. The first thing he taught me was that there are two major forms of the modern language: demotic, which is the people's language, and Katharevousa, or puristic Greek, which was devised by some intellectual Greeks in the early nineteenth century to yoke the modern language to its glorious past. Until the

1970s, Katharevousa was the official language of Greece, used in legal documents and news reporting, although people rarely spoke it. I needed to find a class in demotic Greek and an up-to-date modern-Greek–English dictionary.

Of course, I *could* travel in Greece without Greek, but I kept remembering how on my first venture abroad, on a trip to England, where there is supposedly no language barrier, I felt strangely alienated. In London I didn't know whether to say elevator or lift, apartment or flat. I felt like a phony using the British terms. And the pronunciation—it made me excruciatingly self-conscious to say "shedule" instead of "skedule." What was the point? Wherever I went I was conspicuously American. In Greece I would be doubly alienated. So I registered in NYU's School of Continuing Education for a class in Modern Greek, and *The New Yorker* paid. The magazine routinely covered the tuition for employees who took a class in some subject with a bearing on their work.

The first words I learned in Greek were *ílios*, sun, and *eucharistó*, thank you. To remember words in a foreign language, you make associations with your own tongue, and it thrilled me to realize that the Greek *ílios* had come into English as Helios. What in English is the sun god is, in Greek, the everyday word for the sun. Greek seemed to exalt the everyday. The same with *eucharistó*, from which we get Eucharist, the word for the miracle of the bread and wine becoming the body and blood of Christ. In Greece this word—pronounced "efkhari*sto*"—gets tossed around several times an hour. The English "I thank you" does not carry the reciprocal meaning of a gift both granted and received in the sense that glows out of Eucharist: *eu,* as in Eugenia (well-born) or euphemism (nice, kind, gentle phrase), plus *charis*, from which we get charisma and charism (which religious communities use to mean a particular vocation or gift). In Greek ευχαριστώ seems to indicate a grace and a blessing at every small transaction.

Along with *eucharistó*, thank you, I learned *parakaló*, meaning both please and you're welcome, like the Italian *prego* (beg). I associated *parakaló* with the English word Paraclete, the term used for the Holy Spirit at Pentecost, when the dove descended over the Apostles in the form of licks of flame and gave them the gift of tongues. I did not know there was an etymological source for the association—*parakaló* means literally to call or summon, while Paraclete is the one summoned. For a mnemonic device, I will take anything. Παρακαλώ! Bring it on!

Under Ed's tutelage, I also began to read the classics— Homer and Herodotus—in translation, as well as travel books about modern Greece. Ed piled on the books as if to remake me in his own autodidactic image: Lawrence Durrell, who had lived on Corfu, Rhodes, and Cyprus; Henry Miller, who, as a visitor to Greece before the Second World War, was befriended by the country's greatest living poets; and Patrick Leigh Fermor, a British war hero and travel writer, whose books *Roumeli: Travels in Northern Greece* and *Mani*, about the isolated peninsula in the southern Peloponnese, had a cult following. To top it off, he gave me two precious volumes of poems by Constantine Cavafy, the Alexandrian Greek poet, the pages still uncut, saying as he handed them over, "You'll go farther than I did."

I studied for a year before leaving for Greece, at NYU and then at Barnard. Ed saw me off at the airport, where he initiated me into his preflight ritual: get there early, check in, and start drinking. He was afraid of flying, and suggested we pour libations to Zeus, the sky god, to make sure that the plane had plenty of propellers.

During that maiden voyage to Greece, I made up in five weeks for a childhood confined largely to Ohio. While nursing an ouzo on a ship in the Aegean, mesmerized by the sea, I decided that when I got home I would study classical Greek so that I could read everything written by the Greeks who had crossed this sea before me.

On returning to New York, I registered for Elementary Greek at Columbia University and blithely submitted the bill to the new executive editor, Tony Gibbs, who was the son of Wolcott Gibbs, one of the early *New Yorker* editors. To my disbelief, he turned me down, saying that ancient Greek was not relevant to my job. I had by now moved to the copydesk and I was aghast. I started a dossier of sorts, keeping a list of words from the Greek that cropped up in *The New Yorker*, everything from pi, which is the Greek letter corresponding to "P" and also the mathematical symbol $\pi$—one Greek letter recognized by anyone who had to take geometry in high school—to ophthalmologist, which is often misspelled with a "p" instead of a "ph," the English trans-literation of the Greek letter phi (φ), unless you happen to be fresh from Greek class, where you just learned that the ancient Greek for eye is *ophthalmós*. John McPhee contributed autoch-thonous (*autos*, self, + *chthon*, earth), which means something like self-generated from the earth and contains a tricky com-bination of back-to-back diphthongs in the transliteration of chi (χ) and theta (θ). I loved this stuff!

To reinforce my petition, I asked Eleanor Gould, who was like an oracle to the editors, if she would write a letter attest-ing to the value and relevance of ancient Greek to my job in the copy department. Eleanor wrote that she had not studied Greek in years, so her own knowledge of the language might not be current enough to save us from "ignorant mistakes." It was extremely generous of her, as her knowledge of everything from hanging drapes to reading Russian was more than sufficient. I showed the document to my friend John Bennet, an editor, who said, "You're using a cannon to shoot a flea." Maybe so, but it worked: Tony Gibbs was persuaded that ancient Greek was relevant after all. So it was that in the 1980s I studied classical Greek at Columbia under the aegis of *The New Yorker*.

IN THE YEARS that followed, I swung back and forth between modern Greek and ancient Greek, cramming modern Greek before a trip, returning to ancient Greek when I got home. I moved to Astoria, the Greek-American neighborhood in Queens, embedding myself among live Greeks, and there I consumed Thucydides. I studied one summer at an international program for students of modern Greek in Thessaloniki and played hooky to visit Potidaea, where Socrates served during the Peloponnesian War.

Some people discover a Greek island and go back to the same place again and again, but I always like to go someplace new. I have swum in the Aegean, the Ionian, and the Libyan Seas, taken buses around Lesbos and Thasos and Ithaca, driven to Olympia and Kalamata and Sparta, hopped from island to island in the Dodecanese, a chain named for the twelve major islands (*dodeka*, twelve, + *nisi*, island) along the Turkish coast. I went to Santorini and Naxos with one friend, visited Paros with another friend and went with her to Antiparos (which means Opposite Paros) and to tiny uninhabited Despotiko. One of the most cosmopolitan islands, Mykonos, I avoided for years, but when I got there I understood why people liked it, even though it was crowded and commercial: it was exquisite, a "cubist" town, in Lawrence Durrell's description, the white blocks of buildings tumbling down to the sea, with splashy accents of bougainvillea. I hoped to spend a night on Delos, the uninhabited island that is sacred to Apollo and was the site of the Treasury of the Delian League before the treasure became the federal reserve of the Athenian Empire, but to get permission you had to matriculate in archaeology, in French. I've also gone to some of the far-flung Greek colonies: Napoli, whose name is from the Greek—*neapolis* (new city)—and Siracusa, in the southeastern corner of Sicily, which was the home of Archimedes, the one who shouted "Eureka!" ("I found it!") in the bath when he discovered a way to measure density using what became known as the principle of water displacement.

And so I fell for all things Greek. What is not to love about Greece, after all? There is the sea, the islands, the combination of ancient ruins and cell-phone towers, the guards at the temples who measure their wealth in olive trees, the Old Town of Rhodes, with its streets named for gods and philosophers, navigable by Google Maps. I love the sharp-witted people, the toothless farmers selling long-stemmed artichokes, the black-clad crones linking arms to muscle their way onto ferries ahead of the tourists, the stark contrast between the blues of sea and sky and the whitewashed homes and church domes of the Cyclades, the beads and icons and charms against the evil eye hanging from the bus drivers' rearview mirrors.

I love the landscape of Greece, with its peaks and chasms, its olive groves and orange trees, and the fact that this land has been cultivated since antiquity. I love the animals—the goats and sheep and donkeys, and the crafty cats begging at tavernas, and the stray dogs that sleep in the streets of Athens. The dogs must know far more about the city than any living human, having stored that know-how in their genes and passed it on since the time of Pericles. I love the way the Greeks have squeezed so much out of everything they have: oil from the olive, wine from the grape, ouzo from whatever ouzo is made from—I don't know and I don't care; I'll drink it—feta cheese from sheep's milk and salt, mosaics from pebbles, temples from stone. It is not a rich land, but they have made it rich in ways that transcend a country's gross national product.

I love the mythology, the wealth of stories laid like a series of transparencies over the Old World. The family of gods and goddesses of Olympus—Zeus and Hera and Hermes, Apollo and Artemis and Athena, Poseidon, Ares and Aphrodite and Hephaestus, Hades, Dionysus, Demeter and Persephone—who offer something for everyone. And mythology is not just gods. There are monsters, like the Cyclops, and beings of great majesty, like Pegasus, the winged horse of Bellerophon. There are heroes and victims, whose stories still give us plenty to think about: Odysseus and Achilles, Oedipus and Antigone, Agamemnon and Electra. As background there are the grace notes of nature: a flight of birds seen as an omen of success or failure, a group of rocks or a waterfall commemorating a family tragedy. Above it all, literally, are the stars, blazing with stories, more stories than we can ever tell: Orion the Hunter; the Pleiades, daughters of Atlas; Castor and Polydeuces, the Dioscuri, twin brothers of Clytemnestra and Helen; Cassiopeia on her stiff throne opposite Cepheus, her husband, embodying a minimalist castle; Draco the Dragon.

And most of all I love the language, the ancient slippery

tongue—*glossa!*—from the articles to the epics. Greek isn't easy, though the modern language is at least phonetic: there are no silent "e"s. Learn a few rules and you can pronounce anything (but beware the shifting stress, which can change an innocent adverb into a shocking vulgarity). I still don't know Latin, and in Rome, confronted with inscriptions, I feel illiterate, but in Piraeus I can make out the destinations of the ferries, flashing in light-emitting diodes above the hatch: ΠΑΤΜΟΣ (Patmos), ΚΡΗΤΗ (Crete), ΣΑΝΤΟΡΙΝΗ (Santorini) . . .

Greek has been my salvation. Whenever I have been away from Greek for a while and come back to it, it revives something in me, it gives me an erotic thrill, as if every verb and noun had some visceral connection to what it stands for. I like to think that the first letters were incised into clay and that writing therefore came from the earth. And because the earliest writing to survive was epic poetry, which invokes the gods, writing connects us earthlings to eternity.

A PHILHELLENE WRITING about Greek cannot please everyone. A living Greek or a student of modern Greek may be put off by Greeklish—the transliteration of Greek letters into their English equivalents—as well as by classical Greek, which is laden with diacritical marks. Classicists, on the other hand, look askance at demotic Greek and wonder where the accents went.

In Victorian Britain, when women took up Greek, if they left off an accent their efforts were derided as "ladies' Greek." Shortly after I started studying Greek, in the early eighties, linguists removed the Hellenistic accents from the modern language, retaining only an acute accent to mark a stressed syllable. (They also kept the indispensable diaeresis.)

Every writer on Greek chooses her own way. I admire the restraint of writers who are much better versed in Greek than I am and don't flaunt it. Is there a word of Greek in Edith Hamilton? Or has it all been transliterated? The translator Edmund Keeley, in his book *Inventing Paradise*, about the great modern Greek poets, never gives the reader pause with a foreign-looking word, except in the dedication—and that's not for us anyway. Even a recognizable food word like *tzatziki* might be referred to as yogurt-garlic-cucumber sauce (though a Greek might point out that tzatziki comes from the Turkish).

But sometimes I can't help myself. How can a book about Greek not throw in some actual Greek, like delicious morsels to tempt you to try something ambrosial? You already know more Greek than you think you do. Much of it has passed through the crucible of Latin, but bits of Greek are recognizable in thousands of English words.

And yet Greek is held to be impenetrable, and Greece is treated like the butt of the European Union, dominated by Germany, its citizens the poor cousins of Italy, its economy in perennial crisis. You see more and more English in the neon signs of Athens, and that worries me. While classical Greek flourishes—there is truly a renaissance in translations of Homer—modern Greek may be a dying language. We use names from mythology in every walk of life: the Apollo space mission, the luxurious Hermès scarf, thick Olympus yogurt. I spotted Athena Parking in Los Angeles, City of Angels, which gets its name, through Spanish, from the Greek: άγγελος (*ángelos*), angel, messenger. There is more connecting us to Greek than there is estranging us from it. I wish people weren't intimidated by the Greek alphabet—Greece *gave* us the alphabet (αλφάβητο). Every traveler with a shard of imagination ought to be able to discern from a distance the word TABEPNA and head there confident that in the TAVERNA there will be a narrow straight-backed wicker chair (a little uncomfortable for a big American ass, but you can't have everything) and a glass of ouzo, with ice and water, and something to eat—maybe a plate of tiny fried fish, such as one might feed a seal, or feta cheese cut into cubes the size of dice. And, of course, a cat begging under the table.

As when Ed Stringham, acting as my travel agent, traced a route in the Aegean, conjuring Orthodox monks and Greek sailors and feasts of roast lamb, and opened for me a new world, so I hope to pass the torch by expressing what Greek and Greece have meant to me, both as a perennial student and as a voracious traveler. There is a spell I sometimes fall under in which the whole world looks Greek to me. I hope this book will cast that spell on you. Πάμε, as the Greeks say. Let's go!

# CHAPTER 1

# ALPHA TO OMEGA

〇〇

A FEW YEARS AGO, in the Frankfurt airport on the way home from a memorable stay in Greece, I bought a copy of Virginia Woolf's *The Common Reader*, which includes her essay "On Not Knowing Greek." I had just enough cash in euros for a slim paperback and a giant beer. If not, I would have gone for the beer. I was thirsty, and this was Germany, and I already had a copy of *The Common Reader* at home. But I was impressed that anything by Virginia Woolf was considered airport reading.

I assumed that "On Not Knowing Greek" was about how Woolf's father had forbidden her to study Greek the way my father had refused to let me study Latin. I pictured young Virginia Stephen sulking in a room of her own, an indecipherable alphabet streaming through her consciousness, while her father and her brother, downstairs in the library, feasted on Plato and Aristotle.

Well, apparently I had read only the title of "On Not Knowing Greek." Of *course* Virginia Woolf knew Greek. The essay is a paean to Greek. Her father, Leslie Stephen, was an editor and critic, and Virginia started studying ancient Greek for fun, at home, when she was about fifteen. She took classes at King's College (in the Ladies' Department) while her brother Thoby was studying at Cambridge. Though she was not an academic, she had private tutorials for several years with Miss Janet Case, who, as a student at Cambridge, had played Athena in an 1885 production of the *Eumenides* of Aeschylus, a performance she was remembered for all her life. Together, Miss Case and Miss Stephen (as she was then) read Aeschylus. For Woolf, at the time she published her essay, in 1925, "not knowing Greek" meant that it was impossible truly to know what the playwright meant, because we don't know what the ancient language sounded like. "We can never hope to get the whole fling of a sentence in Greek as we do in English," she writes. In the *Agamemnon*, the opening utterance of Cassandra—the seer, brought to Mycenae from Troy as war booty, whose fate it was never to be believed—is not just untranslatable but unintelligible: ὀτοτοτοῖ is not even a word, just inarticulate syllables that represent a barbarian princess's howl of despair. "The naked cry," Woolf calls it—perhaps onomatopoeia for a convulsive sob. Both the chorus and Clytemnestra compare Cassandra's lament to birdsong. The best an English translation can do is to transliterate the Greek letters—"*Otototoi*"—or go with something like "Ah me!" or "Alas!" Woolf writes that it is "useless . . . to read Greek in translations." Virginia Woolf did not know Greek the way bees do not know pollen. Compared with her, I was a child with a set of wooden blocks that had the letters of the alphabet printed on them, along with apples and bananas. Ὀτοτοτοῖ!

Fortunately, I like blocks, and I love the alphabet. I have a chunky wooden puzzle of the English alphabet, acquired while I was in graduate school, which I meant to give to some child but have kept for myself all these years. I have been known to polish the letters with linseed oil and a soft cloth. I also have the Greek letters in the form of an alphabet book for children, by Eleni Geroulanou, which I bought at the Benaki Museum in Athens, one of the best museums in Greece. It is like the Morgan Library in New York or the Barnes Foundation in Philadelphia or the Isabella Stewart Gardner Museum in Boston in that it houses the collection of an individual with a good eye and ample means—in this case, the Alexandrian Greek Antonis Benakis, who donated his holdings and his family's house to the state in 1931. Instead of apples and bananas and cats, the book's illustrations are of pieces from the collection of the Benaki: alpha is for αεροπλάνο (airplane), beta is for βιβλίο (book), gamma is for γοργόνα (gorgon). I meant to give that to a child, too, at some point, but it cleaves to me.

Anyone who loves language loves the alphabet. Children have a natural affinity for it, and are helped along by such letter-delicacies as Alpha-Bits cereal and alphabet soup. Do you remember how the letters of the alphabet formed a frieze over the blackboard at school when you were a child? Or maybe they danced along the walls, just below the ceiling, each capital paired with its offspring. I used to think of them as mothers and babies. The Big B and the small b were content to go in the same direction, but the small d faced down the Big D. It was defiant—a word I knew from an early age, because my mother frequently said of me, "She's a defiant one."

The word "letter," as in a letter of the alphabet, is also the word for something built of letters, as in a letter home or a letter from a friend, and it is the root of the word literature, which is, ultimately, built of letters of the alphabet. To be lettered is to be literate, and to have letters after your name is to have received a higher education. Children learn to sing the alphabet forwards and backwards. The alphabet is the greatest invention of humankind, and even has a spark of the divine: it gave us the written word, which gave us the means to communicate with both the past and the future. Write it down, we say, when we want to remember something. Write it down and make it stick.

There are other forms of written communication—the Egyptians had hieroglyphs, the Minoans had Linear A to keep track of their food stores, the Native Americans had pictographs, tweeters and texters have emojis and emoticons—but there has never been a system of writing as successful as the alphabet. The magic number, in English, is 26, which is not a small amount of letters to learn when you're a child, but it's not insurmountable, either (especially when it's made into a song), and the combinations of letters that result in meaningful units are infinite. With the alphabet, we can say it long or we can say it short, as when a geneticist invents the term deoxyribonucleic acid and then shrinks it back down to a mere three letters that deliver the same effect: DNA.

The alphabet has chemistry. It might be compared to the periodic table of elements, the way small things stand for large ones and can be used to represent every known material in creation and to synthesize new ones as well. We know where the periodic table came from—Dmitri Mendeleev, a Russian chemist, published it in 1869—but where did the alphabet come from?

The English alphabet is descended from the Greek alphabet, which was derived (as far as anyone can know these things) from the Phoenician alphabet, which had been in use since at least the eleventh century BC. The Phoenicians were famous traders and needed a system to keep track of the merchandise they ferried throughout the Mediterranean. According to Herodotus, the alphabet was imported to Greece by Cadmus, a prince of Phoenicia. Cadmus was the legendary founder of Thebes, a city that was built by warriors who sprang up after Cadmus, on orders from Athena, sowed the earth with the teeth of a dragon.

The earliest Greek alphabetic inscriptions date the alphabet to the eighth century BC. Aeschylus had a different story. He attributes the alphabet to Prometheus: writing, like fire, was a gift from the god. Letters were sacred: inscribed on a shard of pottery, even without being arranged into a name or a coherent thought, they could be offered as a gift at the temple of Zeus.

The alphabet is not just the stuff of mythology; mythology may have been the reason for the alphabet. The Western world's biggest, earliest deposit of mythology is in Homer. The Homeric epics, the *Iliad* and the *Odyssey*, began as an oral tradition and continued as such even after they were written down, sometime around the eighth century BC, about the same time the Greek alphabet was developed. One scholar, Barry B. Powell, suggests the controversial idea that the alphabet may have been invented specifically to set down Homer. Powell asserts that "the *Iliad* was the first work of literature ever recorded in alphabetic writing." It was a new technology, invented by someone who was inspired. Homer is "the earliest alphabetic document in the world," Powell says. Whatever one thinks of Powell's claim, classicists consider the *Iliad* and the *Odyssey* the Bible of the ancient Greek world. From Homer the Greeks got their notions of the gods and the stories that taught people how to deal with the moral dilemmas of war and peace, love and death. The creation of the Greek alphabet was a great awakening.

The Phoenician alphabet that was adapted by the Greeks consisted of twenty-two letters, which were all consonants.

Imagine drawing seven consonants in a game of Scrabble. You would have to channel your inner Phoenician or throw the tiles back and forfeit your turn. The innovation of the Greeks— what made the Greek alphabet such a flexible instrument of expression—was the addition of vowels. A lineup of only vowels in Scrabble would not be ideal, but it would have more potential than all consonants. Vowels are the life and breath of a true alphabet—one in which every sound in the language can be represented by a letter or a combination of letters.

The Greeks initially added just four vowels, including the one at the beginning: alpha (A). Alpha came from aleph, the first letter of the Phoenician alphabet. The sound of aleph was barely a sound at all—more like a grunt, the brief redirection of breath known to linguists as a glottal stop. It creates the hitch in uh-oh. The *American Heritage Collegiate Dictionary* prefaces the entry for the letter A with an illustration of the letter's evolution from the Phoenician—its lineage. Alpha evolved from a pictorial symbol for ox into a representation of a discrete sound. It originally looked like our letter K: the prongs coming off the straight line resembled ox horns. When we say that the Greeks "adapted" the Phoenician alphabet, we mean they messed with it beyond recognition. They flipped the aleph from right to left (a mirror-image K), moved the vertical line to the center, and rotated it, horns and all, ninety degrees to the left: voilà—a crude A. And all this without benefit of a smartphone camera.

Pliny the Elder noted that Palamedes, a hero of the Trojan

War, was sometimes credited with inventing letters to supplement the Phoenician alphabet so as to make it suitable for Greek. In addition to aleph, other Phoenician "gutturals" gave the Greeks names for some of their vowels. The Greek vowel called eta looks like our letter H and represents a long "e" sound (ee), as opposed to the short "e" sound of epsilon. Ayin, which was round like an eye, became omicron—literally, small O.

Later, the Greeks added upsilon, which probably had the sound of "u" (oo) but has slid into an "e" (ee) sound. The very last letter, omega (Ω), literally big O, is one of a handful said to have been invented by Simonides of Ceos, a lyric poet. By the sixth century BC, omega was established, and in 403/2 BC, at the urging of one Eucleides, Athenians voted to replace the old Attic alphabet with the Ionic alphabet, making the omega official.

New consonants were added toward the end of the alphabet, because from the beginning the Greek alphabet doubled as a numerical scheme: alpha = 1, beta = 2, gamma = 3, etc. Mess with that at your peril. Traditionally, the books of the *Iliad* and the *Odyssey* were ordered by letter rather than number. Each epic has the same number of books as there are letters in the Greek alphabet: 24. Thus the alphabet gave structure to the text, and that underlying structure feels like an homage to the alphabet.

The letters of the alphabet don't just float around at random but line up in a well-established order. The order makes the letters easier to learn. What is important, according to The Straight Dope, a newspaper column signed by the fictional Cecil Adams, "isn't what order the alphabet is in, but that it's in order at all." Imagine if everyone in your first-grade class decided to learn the letters in a different order. It would be chaos.

Alphabetical order is remarkably stable: the first two letters have stuck all the way from the Phoenician aleph bet, lending their names to the Greek αλφάβητο and the Roman *alphabetum* and the English alphabet. The only other word I can think of that stands for a set or an order of things and is known by its members is solfège, the system of musical syllables, containing sol and fa, which is also a system for reading, in this case tones instead of words. There are a few theories about what lies behind alphabetical order, some involving shape, some involving sound.

From the very first letters, the Greek alphabet signals the importance of the vowel-consonant relationship: alpha beta. The vowels in both Greek and English are spaced out over the length of the alphabet, like big beads alternating with strings of small beads:

A B Γ Δ E Z H Θ I K Λ M N Ξ O Π P Σ T Υ Φ X Ψ Ω
A B C D E F G H I J K L M N O P Q R S T U V W X (Y) Z

It is the combination of vowels and consonants that makes the alphabet so elastic.

The consonants that were added represented sounds Greeks had that Phoenicians didn't, and they were placed to follow upsilon (Y). The Greek alphabet took over from the Phoenician alphabet as a tool of trade, traveling west in the Mediterranean. Every language that adopted the alphabet adapted it for its own needs. The Etruscans latched on to the Greek alphabet early. Among their contributions was the letter F, repurposing a Greek letter that was pronounced like our W. When the Romans adapted the Etruscan alphabet, they jettisoned several letters because they had no need for them. But during the first century BC the Romans started to use Greek words, so they put back the letters Y and Z, adding the "new" letters to the end.

Anglo-Saxons began to use Roman letters to write Old English when they converted to Christianity in about the seventh century AD. Before that, they used runes. Russians traditionally got their written language when Cyril and Methodius, brothers who were Byzantine monks and missionaries, adapted the Greek alphabet ("perfected" it, the Russians say), adding letters to represent Slavic sounds. Hence it is called the Cyrillic alphabet.

In this way, the original Phoenician aleph bet was shaped, sometimes by a single person, into a system of writing that transcended its commercial usefulness and made it into a tool for the preservation of memory, for recording history and making art: a gift of the Muses and for the Muses.

ONE WAY OF MASTERING the letters in the Greek alphabet is to think of them as characters. A "character" is a symbol for recording language. On Twitter, you originally had to limit your remarks to 140 characters, including all punctuation and spaces between words. (The limit was later doubled to 280 characters, a decision of dubious merit.) The word comes from the ancient Greek *charásso*, meaning to "make sharp, cut into furrows, engrave." The leap from a symbol graved in stone to a person endowed with a sharply defined personality is a good example of the way a word ripples out into metaphor.

Can a character, as in a letter of the alphabet, have a character, in the abstract sense of a distinct trait? Certain associations have grown up around the letters that are used as grades in school: A is excellent, B is not as good as A (the B list, a B movie), C is average, D is disappointing, and F is failure, a mark of shame. Then again A is for adultery; it is the scarlet letter with which Nathaniel Hawthorne branded Hester Prynne. Superman has a big red S. Vladimir Nabokov devotes a few paragraphs in his autobiography, *Speak, Memory* (its title an invocation to the mother of the Muses), to the colors he associates with letters of the alphabet: his "blue group" includes "steely *x*, thundercloud *z*, and huckleberry *h*." He goes on, "Since a subtle interaction exists between sound and shape, I see *q* as browner than *k*, while *s* is not the light blue of *c*, but a curious mixture of azure and mother-of-pearl. . . . The word for rainbow . . . is in my private language the hardly pronounceable: *kzspygv*." I think we can agree that Nabokov was hallucinating and stick to an English mnemonic for the colors of the rainbow, Roy G. Biv, an acronym for *r*ed *o*range *y*ellow *g*reen *b*lue *i*ndigo *v*iolet.

Greek letters have their own mystique. Outside of an encounter with pi (π) in geometry class, I did not see Greek characters until I got to college and was puzzled by the symbols attached to the facades of fraternity houses: a gigantic X (chi), a pitchfork Ψ (psi), an impenetrable Φ (phi). No one who is not a member of the fraternity is privy to the secret motto that the characters stand for. Still, if these are the only Greek letters that people are likely to encounter, it is worth looking at "Greek life" as a way into Greek letters.

The first Greek fraternity in America was founded at William and Mary College in 1776, by a student named John Heath. He had supposedly been rejected from a study group with a Latin name, and his response was to found his own study group and give it a Greek name—that would show them. Greek has more snob appeal than Latin. So he formed Phi Beta Kappa. Its members were students of upstanding character who studied hard and got good grades. Phi Beta Kappa (ΦΒΚ) stood for Philosophia Biou Kybernetes: "The love of wisdom is the guide of life." "*Philo*" + "*sophia*" is "love of wisdom"; in "*Kybernetes*" you can almost make out the word "govern" (through Latin *guberno*, to steer); and "*Biou*" is the genitive form of "bio," life, as in biology (the study of life) and biography (the writing of a life). The copulative verb—"is"—is understood.

Frat boys and sorority girls take their vow of secrecy very seriously. I could persuade only one Greek society, of honors English majors, called Sigma Tau Delta (ΣΤΔ), to reveal its motto to me—Sincerity, Truth, Design. Perhaps this transparency helps to distance its members from the ready association with its English initials: STD.

The fictional Delta Tau Chi (ΔTX) is as nearly the opposite of Phi Beta Kappa as a fraternity can be, its members known as animals for their wild behavior, which supplied the name for both their campus digs and the movie: *Animal House*. If we knew what secret motto lurked behind those letters (Drink to Excess?), we would have a link between the Greek characters and the characters portrayed in the film.

I have a couple of books about the alphabet—one about the Greek alphabet and two about the English alphabet—but even to an alphabetophile like me these books get boring somewhere around "D is for Delta." They are just too predictable—we know how the alphabet ends—and one begins to gasp for air between K and L, which is not quite halfway. So let's skip on down to the end, where the Greeks added the three consonants they needed for sounds the Phoenicians did not have. One is phi, which sounds like *f* but is usually transliterated in ancient Greek as *ph*. Philip of Macedon, the father of Alexander the Great, was Philippos in Greek: lover (*philos*) of horses (*hippos*). A hippopotamus is a horse of the river.

Another such character is psi, which may be my favorite letter. It can be found at the beginning of every English word that is a variant on psyche: psychology, psychotherapy, psychiatry, psychoanalyst, psychosomatic, psychopath, psychopharmacopeia, all descended from Psyche, the lover of Eros, who was the son of Aphrodite. The psi looks like a trident, attribute of Poseidon, god of the sea, and it is the first letter in the modern Greek word for fish: ψάρι (*psári*).

The third is chi, the one that looks like an X but is most often transliterated as the hard *ch* in chaos. It is the trickster of the Greek alphabet. It is not the same as our English X—no way. For that, the Greeks have a completely different letter, xi (Ξ). Speakers of English often have trouble pronouncing words with *ch* in them—melancholy, chalcedony, chiropodist, chimera—because *ch* also represents the sound in such common English words as church, chicken, and cheese. (You could say our alphabet is imperfect.) To be fair, Greeks cannot pronounce our *ch*, which is why, in the classic Greek-diner skits on the old *Saturday Night Live*, John Belushi always called out, "Tseezbourger, tseezbourger, tseezbourger."

Some translators prefer to skip over the Roman tradition and write chi as *kh*, for more of a Greek flavor. We are used to seeing the Roman spelling of Achilles, but the name appears in some translations of the *Iliad* and the *Odyssey* as Akhilleus. In modern Greek, the consonant sound of chi is a cross between *k* and *h*, like the *ch* of the Hebrew words Chanukah and Chasidic. Some people lack the chutzpah to pronounce that sound and are unable to ask you to pass the challah. Sometimes, chi is transliterated with an *h* instead of a *ch,* again as in Hebrew: Hanukkah, Hasidic. So this chi that looks like X takes three forms in English: *ch, kh,* and *h.* When the transliterating goes in the opposite direction, for instance, when a Greek wants to spell out the name Hilton, as in the Athens Hilton, he might go with Chilton. An American might laugh at that—it's against company policy—and the sound of laughter in Greek is spelled with chi: χα-χα.

The character that looks like X has a nonalphabetical use that is common to both languages. According to *Scribes and Scholars,* a study by L. D. Reynolds and N. G. Wilson of how Greek and Roman literature was preserved and transmitted through the ages, one of the ways that scholars at the Library of Alexandria notated a point of textual interest was by writing the letter chi in the margin. A penciled-in X is still the mark that a conservative reader—that is, one who prefers not to deface a book—puts in the margin next to a line he wants to revisit.

Many of the surviving works of the Greeks—including Homer, Aeschylus, Sophocles, Euripides, Aristophanes, Herodotus, and Aristotle—have come down to us in the form we have them thanks to the work of the diligent librarians of Alexandria, who, beginning around 280 BC, under Ptolemy Philadelphus, established the canon. If it were not for the ancient librarians, we would not have this trove of books.

According to the *Oxford Companion to Classical Literature*, Aristophanes of Byzantium, the head librarian around 200 BC, purportedly invented or regularized the diacritical marks that are such a headache for students of the classics. The librarians cataloged and classified and established authenticity and published authoritative editions. Imagine, the *Oresteia* of Aeschylus squeaked through in a single degraded manuscript! The first play in this masterly trilogy, *Agamemnon*, had to be pieced together from fragments. Librarians encouraged a tradition of respect for literature, working to conserve the texts in their original form. Known as scholiasts, they were among the first editors and scholars and literary critics; their annotations, still studied today, are often longer than the works themselves.

When I worked as a sort of scribe (which is a very hard job, by the way, nowhere near as easy as it looks, fraught with perils) in the collating department of *The New Yorker*, William Shawn would sometimes put an X with a circle around it in the margin of a galley proof to indicate a query that he wanted us to carry over to the next version of the piece. The query might be important, but he did not yet have enough information to address it. We scribes would circle that query in blue and set the page aside to copy onto the next day's proof, to remind Mr. Shawn to ask the author about it. If the collator put the query directly into the piece, or if the editor tried to make a fix without being sure what the author meant, there was a danger of corrupting the text.

It is conceivable that X is the original, maybe even the

aboriginal, written mark. X marks the spot, as it says on all the treasure maps. Its crossed bars create a fixed point. X is also the traditional signature of an illiterate—laboriously scratched out by a cowboy before, with his last spasm, he kicks the bucket—so it is both precise and general: anyone can sign his name with an X. It may be the most useful symbol of all. How did the Phoenicians get along without it? X equals the unknown.

IF YOU THINK GREEK is hard to read now, you should have seen it when the Greeks were just starting out. They had only the capital letters—small letters were developed in the Middle Ages, to speed up writing and save on parchment. I am reluctant to refer to the small letters as "lowercase," because that term—as well as uppercase, for capital letters—comes from movable type and is anachronistic. Printers organized type into drawers, or cases, and kept the capitals in a higher case and reached down into a case below the upper case for the small letters; ergo lowercase. The uppercase and lowercase letters are also called by the Latinate terms majuscule and minuscule (major and minor).

Greeks did not put any spaces between the words, SOTH-EREADERHADTOFIGUREOUTWHEREONEWOR-DLEFTOFFANDTHEOTHERBEGAN. At first, they wrote from right to left, like the Phoenicians (Hebrew is still written from right to left), but then they switched and wrote from left to right. This probably accounts for the backward orientation of some of the letters, like that aleph that went from a K to a backwards K before settling into alpha: A. For a while, they wrote in both directions: they might start out writing from left to right, and when they ran out of room they would work their way back from right to left, and then turn from left to right again. This manuscript style is called boustrophedon: *bous* (ox) + *strophe* (turn)—"as the ox turns," referring to the way an ox and plow go back and forth across a field. The metaphor suggests some deep connection between writing and the earth.

Spacing is still controversial. Though in modern typography it is generally agreed that one space after a period is enough, there are people who would sooner have their thumbs cut off than give up their right to double-space. Copy editors can guess the age of a writer by his or her typing habits. Those who double-space after a period went to college in the late sixties, early seventies, or earlier, and used a portable typewriter that was a gift from their parents. *The New Yorker,* in the days of hot type, put two spaces after a period, but when word processers came in, around 1994, the first thing the editorial staff learned was "one space after a period." Wide spacing has its charms, not the least of which is that it creates jobs for people who remove the extra space.

A few other trends actually seem to be moving backward in the new millennium. For instance, audiobooks are a return to the oral tradition, and podcasts—talks, interviews, radio series—

dispense with the written record completely. The codex—the book with turnable pages sewn between covers—was a great improvement over the scroll, but now, with publication online, we are back to scrolling again, which makes it hard to refer back to things. And vowels, the innovation of some god or genius, are now playfully omitted, as if they took up too much space. Someone might write "srsly" online (but not in print), creating a (sltly) humorous effect, or sign off with a distinctive "yrs" instead of the more formal "Yours." (But no one would dare write "sncrly yrs"—the sentiment is insincere without vowels.) There is a chain of restaurants called GRK, like an abbreviation for an airport, and no one would mistake it for Gork or Grak. People know that here they can get a Greek salad (or GRK sld). A banner outside a church building in New York that was converted into a nightclub called the Limelight, and later into a mall and then a gym, floats the letters MNSTR, leaving one to choose between "monster" and "minister," and giving no clue what goes on in the building anymore. Who among Phoenicians knew that their alphabet would one day triumph as a marketing gimmick?

Spacing is basically a negative form of punctuation, and it was a great leap forward. Actual marks in the text to help the reader were minimal—a raised dot or two were used to indicate a change of speaker in a play, and there are still arguments over whether a line in, say, the *Prometheus* belongs to Io or the chorus. Aristophanes of Byzantium gets the credit for using a system of dots to suggest pauses in speech. As Keith Houston recounts in

*Shady Characters*, his book about the history of punctuation, the dot was placed in the middle of the line for a short pause (a comma), at the bottom of the line for a longer pause (a colon), and at the top for a full stop (the period). The modern Greek word for a period is *teleía*, related to the verb "to finish, complete, perfect." The comma comes from the Greek word *komma*, meaning something cut off, a segment. Its form did not solidify until the Renaissance, when printers made sumptuous new editions of Greek works. The comma was created to prevent confusion. Punctuation has always had the reader's welfare at heart. Ancient Greek has clues right in the words—inflections, tweaks to the spelling—that sometimes make punctuation unnecessary. But would it have killed them to put a period at the end of a sentence?

SOMETIMES, when I was studying Greek on *New Yorker* time, I'd mix up my alphabets and my dictionaries and open *Webster's* when I meant to consult Liddell and Scott—the Greek-English lexicon. I'd flip to the end and be surprised to see the letter Z instead of omega. What is that doing here? I'd wonder, before remembering that I was not in Athens, ancient or modern, but in midtown Manhattan, working in American English.

I don't mean to demean the letter Z. What would we do without it? The bees would not buzz, the zoo would close forever, the zigzag would lose its zing. The English alphabet seems to run out at the end in a way that the Greek alphabet does not. The letter Z has the feel of an afterthought, which is exactly what it was when the Romans, who had plucked it out of the Greek alphabet in the first place, restored it by pinning it back on at the end, like a tail on the alphabetum.

In the Greek alphabet, zeta comes sixth, between epsilon and eta. Its name follows the pattern of beta, and it kicks off the pleasing sequence "zeta eta theta." Both alphabets get a little shaky toward the end. I always have to sing the whole alphabet song to remember the sequence of the letters between QRS and XYZ. The Greek alphabet opens up after Greek Y—upsilon—and tucks in those three consonants that the Phoenician aleph bet lacked and the Greeks could not do without—phi, chi, psi (the order does not come naturally to me)—before crowning the alphabet with omega. Remember that the alphabet song, set to the same tune as "Twinkle, Twinkle, Little Star" and "Baa Baa Black Sheep," does not actually end at the letter Z, but goes on to fill out the cadence with the rather lame "Now I know my ABC's. Next time, won't you sing with me." If you were in my second-grade class, you went on to sing the alphabet backwards, proving total mastery, and maybe absorbing the fact that alphabetical order does not necessarily imply a hierarchy.

Z is still called zed in British English, probably a holdover from the Greek zeta. It is thanks to Noah Webster that

Americans call it zee instead of zed. Webster knew a thing or two about alphabets—he studied dozens of languages before compiling the great American dictionary. He also knew about pedagogy—how to teach children—having started out as a schoolteacher; his first dictionary was conceived as a spelling aid for grammar schools. Webster would not have attempted to change the order of the alphabet—that would be madness—but he did suggest some improvements.

Rhyme makes things easier to memorize (zeta eta theta), and Webster thought it might better serve the cause of literacy to change the names of certain letters in the English alphabet. H (aitch) would more logically be called "he," following the pattern of B, C, D, E, and representing its consonant sound. H has a convoluted history as a consonant. In Greek it's a vowel, eta. The letter got broken down and its upper extremities were used to create breathing marks—rough (') and smooth (')—that look like single quotation marks perched over initial vowels. And W (double U) is completely wrong: I remember looking at it in kindergarten and thinking, But that's a double V. Webster wanted to simplify W by calling it "we." (In ancient times, the Greek alphabet had the digamma for the sound of W, but it disappeared sometime after the fall of Troy and hasn't been heard from since, except in remote scholarly regions—and among the Etruscans.) For similar reasons, Webster thought that Y (why) might better be called "yi." What a nut. None of these innovations caught on, but by the time Webster got to the end of the alphabet he seems to have worn down the opposition. He succeeded in getting Americans to refer to the ultimate character as zee instead of zed.

Things that come first and last are in especially emphatic positions. In English, we use the expression A to Z to mean everything you need to know—about fashion, fundraising, sex—in a prescribed and predictable order. A theater critic might write that an actress "ran the gamut of emotions from A to Z," meaning that by the end she was all out, empty, exhausted. Our alphabet runs out of steam. But the Greek alphabet is different. It ends not with a seldom-used consonant but with a big fat vowel: omega, big O, Ω, ω. Oh! Omega has energy in it, it has breath and inspiration. Omega sends you back to the vowel at the beginning, to the alpha, in a way that Z just doesn't, and picks up overtones from the vowel in the middle, the omicron, or small O. The very shape of the omega is open at the end. The Greek alphabet, like Greek syntax, does not seem linear: it feels round. Nobody seriously translates "I am the Alpha and the Omega," the words of the Almighty from the Book of Revelation, as "I am A through Z." The Greek alphabet is infinite.

# CHAPTER 2

# A IS FOR ATHENA

๏๏

M Y FIRST EXPOSURE to Greek mythology was at the
Lyceum—not the famed Lykeion in Athens, where
Aristotle and his pupils strolled around as they discussed philoso-
phy and beauty, but a movie theater on Fulton Road in Cleveland,
where my brothers and I spent Saturday afternoons. The Lyceum
was classic as opposed to classical: popcorn in red-and-white striped
boxes, a stern lady usher who confiscated the candy we snuck in
from outside, buzzers under the seats for a gimmicky thrill.

Every week, the Lyceum showed a double feature, usually
a horror movie—*The Mummy, Godzilla, The Creature from the
Black Lagoon*—paired with something mildly pornographic
(and highly educational). At one Saturday matinee, I laid eyes
for the first time on the Cyclops. The movie was *Ulysses* (1955
AD), starring Kirk Douglas as the man of many turnings. In
a way, it, too, was a horror movie, full of monsters and appari-

tions: a witch who turned men into pigs, sea serpents, Anthony Quinn in a short tight skirt.

Ulysses is the Latinate name for Odysseus and the one preferred by Hollywood and James Joyce. How Odysseus became Ulysses is, like many things that happened between Greece and Rome, impossible to say for sure. Scholars have suggested that the "D," or delta, of Odysseus in Ionic Greek was originally an "L," or lambda, in the Dorian and Aeolic dialects. Delta (Δ) and lambda (Λ) are similar in form—a wedge with or without a bar—but to my knowledge no one has suggested that Odysseus was the ancient equivalent of a typo for Ulysses. The name may have reached Rome independently as Ulixes through Sicily, the traditional home of the Cyclops.

In Catania, a city under Mount Etna built largely of polished black lava, souvenir shops sell ceramic figurines of the Cyclops. The Cyclopes (plural) were a race of giants, similar to the Titans, clumsy prototypes for human beings. Polyphemus worked on Mount Etna, forging lightning bolts for Zeus. A friend from Catania told me some Sicilians believe that the Cyclops *was* Mount Etna, which erupted like Polyphemus' eye after Odysseus poked it with a pointed stick, spewing into the sea stones that formed the Faraglioni di Acitrezza, dramatic stacked rocks in the Gulf of Catania. At any rate, one can imagine the story of the Cyclops going out into the world ahead of the epic poem, the way the Cyclops episode in the movie at the Lyceum preceded my knowledge of Homer. There is nothing like an old-fashioned Cyclops to get your attention.

Athena must have appeared in the movie—what is the *Odyssey* without Athena? She is the protector of Ulysses; he would not survive without her. Surely the hero invokes her—I must have heard her name. But I don't recall meeting Homer's gray-eyed goddess at the Lyceum. No tomes of mythology by Bulfinch, the d'Aulaires, or Edith Hamilton sat on the bookshelves in our house—in fact, there were no bookshelves in our house. But we had comic books and library cards, and I subsisted happily on the Brothers Grimm and Little Lulu. I did not, like a prodigy, read the *Iliad* in translation at fourteen. I had a weakness for the genre of the girl detective, for Nancy Drew and Trixie Belden. I also liked Poe and Dickens and Mark Twain and tried to read Hawthorne (yawn) and Sir Walter Scott (snore) and Dostoyevsky (coma). Anything I learned about Greek mythology was either absorbed through popular culture or through writers in English. In junior year at Lourdes Academy, the all-girls Catholic high school I attended in Cleveland, we read Joyce's *Portrait of the Artist as a Young Man*, the lesson of which, according to Sister Diane Branski, was that though Joyce had lost his faith (and left Ireland), he could never get away from the Church (or Dublin). And neither would we.

Perhaps the spirit of Athena hovered over Lake Erie, but in those days—the fifties and sixties, when the twentieth century still felt like the future—my primary model, like that of most girls in the normal course of things, was my mother. She cooked, made the beds, swept the floor. She was a world-class talker—"Your mom sure has the gift of gab," people would say—and she sang as she washed the dishes, songs like "Fascination" and "I've Got You Under My Skin." But to me washing the dishes was nothing to sing about. And while her example was powerful—as a nine-year-old, I fantasized about having a toy carpet sweeper—I was dubious about following in her footsteps. For one thing, she rarely went anywhere.

My mother and I were outnumbered by the males in the family, and I disliked being grouped with her. I felt housebound. I remember the taste of the front door, which I pressed my tongue against in my desperation to get outside—harsh cold glass in winter, bitter metallic screen in summer. I was always comparing my mother with other girls' mothers, wishing to trade up. The nuns gave me models other than my mother, and I had an inkling that I might be popular in the convent. I liked the idea of changing my name—it would be a fresh start—but I worried about having to get up early, at the gong of a bell, and go to Mass every day. The convent was something to fall back on in case I didn't get married. I had a feeling I wasn't going to get married. But the nun's life seemed just as circumscribed as my mother's.

Once, for sixth-grade religion class, we were split into groups for a project on vocations. The nun handed out pamphlets describing what could be expected from each calling: you got married, you became a priest or a nun, or you remained single. I was put on the "single" panel. Remaining single did not feel like a choice—it was something you got stuck with, like the unmated card in a game of Old Maid. But the pamphlet pointed out that although you might not choose it, if you were to die tomorrow—tragically, at age twelve—you would perforce be single. The only divine model the Church offered a girl was the Blessed Virgin Mary.

I suppose Athena became a model to me without my even realizing it: a third way. Athena, like Mary, is a virgin—*parthénos*—but she does not carry the paradoxical burden of maternity. She was born, fully formed and armed for battle, a warrior, from the head of Zeus. Her mother, by most accounts, was Metis, one of the Titans, rivals of the Olympians, meaning that Athena came from old stock. Because Metis wasn't around (I am sorry to report that Zeus swallowed her while she was pregnant), Athena had none of the conflicts a girl has with her mother. She gets along well with Zeus's wife, Hera, that most irritable of goddesses. Zeus never pressures her to marry.

Other women and girls may favor a different goddess. Many opt for Artemis, the huntress; someone who longs for children might identify with Demeter; great beauties are chosen by Aphrodite. Hera is not popular; in her Roman guise as Juno she is statuesque and confident, but what a bitch. For me, it had to be Athena. Whereas the Virgin Mary is a model of humility and servitude, Athena is the template for a liberated woman.

Athena is unfettered: she has no masculine deity to accommodate, no children to appease, no family obligations to juggle with her career. She is beholden to no one—Zeus treats her with respect and indulgence. Like a favorite daughter, she knows how to handle him. He trusts her judgment and lets her have her way. Her virginity may be one of the reasons Athenians chose her to be the patron of their city: she would be dedicated. The founding myth of Athens is that Athena and Poseidon were rivals for top honors in the city. Athena planted an olive tree on the Acropolis, and Poseidon caused salt water to spring up on its slopes. The gods judged the olive the greater gift and awarded the city to Athena.

Not that Athena doesn't have domestic virtues: she is a weaver and a patron of the crafts, a civilizing influence. She's not a fertility goddess, like Demeter and Artemis, but more of a survivor. Olive trees are legendarily resilient. Chop one down or burn it up, and new shoots grow from the stump. And Athena didn't just plant that olive tree—someone had to impart the knowledge of how to cultivate it and how to press from its hard, bitter green fruit the precious essence of what the earth has to offer. Olive oil is an ingredient in everything from salads to shampoo, and the Greeks even used it as fuel, burning it in lamps. Athena seems to me to be the great example of using your resources wisely.

Most of all, Athena has tremendous feminine strength. In the *Iliad*, when Zeus lets the gods take up arms along with the mortals on the battlefield, Athena lays out Ares flat—Ares, the god of war! Athena can be terrifying. She wears the head of Medusa on her breast, at the center of her shield, or aegis. The Gorgon's head was a gift from Perseus, who slew the monster while looking at her reflection in his shield instead of directly at her face, which would have turned him to stone. In art history, Medusa leers comically from a round frame: snaky locks for hair, tusks, a pig's snout for a nose. She sticks out her tongue at you. The message is "Don't mess with me, you weakling."

Athena is direct: she never tries to seduce anyone or wheedle to get her way. Her brand of wisdom is a form of common sense, which was something I lacked, a muscle that did not get much exercise in college or graduate school. I was a good worker, though—the only job I ever had that I was truly terrible at was waiting on tables—and by the time I got to *The New Yorker* there were different kinds of women to observe: a cheerful receptionist heading back to graduate school, proofreaders of all styles—zealous, jealous, quietly brilliant—and wickedly good writers, like Pauline Kael and Janet Malcolm. When I was promoted to the copydesk, my dream job, and it was just me and the words, I had a crisis of confidence. No one thanked you when you did something right, but when you screwed up they had ways of letting you know.

The copydesk was like a sieve for prose: the copy editor filtered out impurities without adding anything new. I swung back and forth between extremes, trying to do less rather than more while also trying not to draw attention to myself by missing anything egregious. I wanted to write, so I was envious when one of my contemporaries at the office succeeded in placing a story in The Talk of the Town. When I copy-edited a colleague's work, I had to filter out my own impurities. One evening I ran into William Shawn in the elevator vestibule. "You look troubled," he said. Probably I was worried about having to share an elevator with Mr. Shawn, but I told him I was not sure I would ever master my job on the copydesk. He gave me a steady look—we were almost the same height; he was five foot five, and his eyes were at the same level as mine—and assured me that I would learn by osmosis.

Athena turned out to be a good model for a copy editor. She wouldn't worry about offending a writer or whether a writer liked her or not, and she wouldn't let anyone get away with anything. I just had to trust that my motives were pure: I was there for the language. Once I'd absorbed the ethos of copy editing, and moved from the copydesk, where you couldn't correct things even when you knew they were wrong, to the next level, among the copy editors I most admired—page O.K.'ers, in *The New Yorker*'s terminology—I stopped worrying so much. At a museum, I was attracted to a print of a Gorgon, leering comically with her tongue stuck out. I bought that print and pinned it up over my desk.

ATHENA APPEARS IN Book 2 of the *Odyssey* as Mentor, a friend to whom Odysseus entrusted the care of his son when he left Ithaca for Troy. The word mentor, meaning counselor or teacher, comes to us directly from Homer. It is thousands of years old. William Shawn was acting as a mentor when he spoke to me in the vestibule, counseling patience. Sometimes all it takes is a hint, like a drop of iodine in a glass of water, to tint your view of things and help you see the way forward. As a child, I had a pattern of making friends with girls who had older sisters—a big sister would have made all the difference to me. As I got older, my mentors got younger. They just had to be people who had more experience than I did. But, crucially, a mentor has to choose you. You can't force someone to take you on.

There was a tradition of mentoring in the copy department at *The New Yorker*—one of the veterans took it upon herself to train the next generation—but sometimes it felt as if I were learning how to navigate between Scylla and Charybdis. Scylla was Eleanor Gould, a genius, someone it was impossible to emulate because you couldn't possess her formidable intelligence. Charybdis was Lu Burke, a taskmaster, who hurled dictionaries at people's heads. Away from the office, as I got deeper into Greek, I found a gentler mentor in a woman at Barnard who agreed to tutor me in modern Greek. Her name was Dorothy Gregory. She was the best teacher I've ever had.

Dorothy was petite, with dark hair and eyes, a sharp chin, and a sweet, archaic smile, as if she were amused at something from a vast distance. She was always well dressed: tweed skirt,

wool sweater, belted coat. She was generous, often compliment-
ing people. "You look like a model," she'd say, though not to me.
"You always come running," she observed once when I arrived at
her office breathless after rushing uptown from work.

Dorothy was from Corfu, which is in the Ionian Sea, west
of mainland Greece. She had lived in Michigan and Indone-
sia and done graduate work at Columbia, specializing in Walt
Whitman. This makes sense in retrospect: Whitman is our most
rhapsodic poet, and Dorothy loved the work of the Nobel Prize–
winning Greek poet Odysseus Elytis, who rhapsodized about all
the islands in the Aegean and all the regions of Greece and their
people. *Rhapsodós*, ῥαψῳδός, means a stitcher of songs, from
ῥάπτω, to sew, and ᾠδή, ode. It was the word for someone who
recited epic poetry in ancient times. In modern Greek, ῥάφτης
(*ráftis*) means tailor—a word that stuck with me, so that once,
in Thessaloniki, coming upon a writer friend who was sewing a
button onto his shirt in the lobby of a hotel, I could say, with
authority, "Ο ῥάφτης"—"The tailor." Rhapsodic has a sense of
wonder in English that comes from the poet's engagement with
the material.

Dorothy was endlessly patient with me, and indulgent of
my desire to learn this immensely complex tongue and one day
dance on a table in emulation of Zorba the Greek.

Sometimes Dorothy made me feel as if *I* were the mentor in
this relationship. Once, crossing the street, I noted that we were
jaywalking. "What did you say?" Dorothy said.

"Jaywalking. It's when you cross against the light." I'm not sure where it comes from, but I always associated it with jail.

"*Jaywalking!*" she repeated. "You taught me something!"

Greek was my therapy in those days, my relief from my native tongue and the life that went with it. I wrote stilted paragraphs on such topics as washing my clothes at the laundromat: I aired my dirty linen on paper. I could be unspeakably vulgar in my adopted tongue, as when I reported on a trip to the pharmacy with my friend Clancey in search of cough medicine, and the pharmacist asked whether I needed an expectorant or a suppressant: " 'Cough for the man,' Clancey told me. I did."

Dorothy laughed. The Greek word *káno*, like the French *faire* and the Italian *fare*, means both "I do" and "I make," and does not do double duty as a reinforcing verb, the way it does in English. The past tense, έκανα, is what Greek children holler from the toilet ("I made!") when they have had a bowel movement.

So much of language study is learning *not* to say things.

But most of the time it was exhilarating, and my notebooks filled with new vocabulary. Dorothy taught me a little modern Greek history, including the legend of Bouboulina, a woman who commanded a fleet during the War of Independence, in 1821. She explained the rituals of Orthodox Easter, when families roast a lamb on a spit over coals in the yard. I was taken by the custom of tapping together red-dyed hard-boiled eggs—whoever's egg doesn't crack is the winner. I asked Dorothy why the Greeks dye their eggs only the color red, and her first response was to wonder why we in the West dye our eggs all those dull pastels when a vibrant red is the obvious choice. "Red is the color of blood and the color of joy," she said.

It was while I was first studying with Dorothy that I read the *Iliad*, in Robert Fitzgerald's translation. Before that, I had preferred the *Odyssey* and found war stories punishing. I noticed that every time the Achaeans, as Homer calls the Greeks, need to propitiate the gods and sacrifice hecatombs of oxen, supposedly so that the gods can savor the odor of grilled meats (the gods have no need for food, subsisting on ambrosia), it is an excuse for a feast. They share out the meat, family style, as in a Greek restaurant, or turn chunks on a spit—the original souvlaki, or "little skewer," diminutive of *soúvla*, as prepared on street corners in Astoria. They pour libations to the gods before taking a drink themselves. I started making a practice of pouring libations, splashing beer into a potted plant or, to my dinner companions' horror, spilling expensive wine over the rail of the porch at an elegant outdoor restaurant. The Greeks offered libations to the gods to thank them or to ask for their blessing. Maybe it was just an excuse to drink, but pouring the first sip onto the earth or into the sea, giving the gods the first taste, became a habit, a way of saying grace, the ritual prayer before a meal (*Bless us O Lord and these Thy gifts which we are about to receive from Thy bounty through Christ our Lord Amen*). If you accidentally knock over a glass, good: it's a spontaneous libation. Sometimes, a libation is more of a gesture than a generous pour, as when you are on an airplane and with moistened fingertip flick a drop toward the carpeting, hoping not to stain the pants leg of the gentleman next to you. I invoke the good will of whatever god is most appropriate to my current project: Zeus for air travel, Hermes for a road trip, Apollo for a doctor's visit or for self-discipline, Hephaestus for engine trouble and for all plumbing emergencies, and always, always Athena for guidance.

One day in Dorothy's office, catching my breath as we settled into a lesson on the future perfect, I felt strangely excited. I looked at Dorothy, bent over the desk, sketching a paradigm in my notebook (she often took notes for me), and found myself wondering . . . I developed crushes on male teachers all the time, but here I was feeling an erotic attraction to a woman. The room was warm and I was breathing heavily. Steam was coming off me. I decided it was the language that thrilled me—Greek is sexy.

THAT SPRING, I made my first trip to Greece. It was an ambitious itinerary. Originally, I thought I'd go from island to island, in emulation of Odysseus, but the *Iliad*, set on the shores of what is now Turkey, had made me aware of Asia Minor and the Greek presence there throughout history, and I wanted to search for Homer in the theater of the Aegean. Ed Stringham had taught me that Greece looks east, toward Asia, not west toward the rest of Europe. On the night ferry from Piraeus to Crete,

I got up early and went out on deck to catch Homer's famed *rhododáctylos,* the rosy fingers of dawn. I was hoping for a glorious display in the east to welcome me to the Mediterranean. The only other passengers on deck were a few men leaning against the rail, smoking cigarettes, and a black-clad crone huddled in the stairwell, holding her kerchief over her face, seasick. (The Greeks are famously prone to seasickness—they could even be said to have invented it. The word "nausea" comes from the ancient Greek *naus,* for "ship.") The sky was overcast, but I stayed on deck, shivering, eyes on the horizon, waiting for a sign from the gods. One of the men offered me a cigarette as we neared the harbor of Heraklion. At last, a pink smudge appeared among the clouds and then got rubbed out. That was it: I had to settle for the rosy knuckle of dawn.

There was something I did not understand on that trip, and on several subsequent trips (and readings of Homer), and figured out only at home, in New York. I woke up one day and rolled over to look out the window, as usual, to see if the early morning light was turning the tops of the buildings pink—a phenomenon I enjoy so much that I have never hung a curtain at my bedroom window—and sat up sharp. *Rhododáctylos* (from *rhodos,* rose, and *dactylos,* finger) refers not to a display of slender pink fingers stretched out along the eastern horizon but to what those fingers touch: the tall things first, water towers and skyscrapers. Think of Midas or, in our day, Goldfinger: he did not himself have fingers of gold, but anything he touched turned to gold. As Adam Nicolson puts it in *Why Homer Matters*, "Everyone knows that Homeric dawn is 'rosy-fingered'—not rayed with her outspread fingers, but touching the tips of trees and rocks with her fingers."

I didn't stay in any one place too long on that first trip. It was (and sometimes still is) my style of travel to go to great lengths to get someplace and then decide that just getting there was enough: let's leave. I grew up in Cleveland with a father who believed, based on his experiences in the army in the Second World War, that one place was much like another and there was no point in going anywhere new, because it wouldn't be any different. In other words, you take yourself with you wherever you go.

So I shot around the Aegean like a pinball: from Crete to Rhodes, Cyprus, Samos, Chios, Lesbos. In a couple of weeks of travel, I got hit on by waiters, flirted with by a deckhand and a petty officer, and courted by a college English professor. On the ferry from Piraeus I had accepted a cigarette from a man named Mimi, a diminutive of Dmitri, who farmed tomatoes on the southern coast of Crete. He offered to show me Knossos, the excavated remains of the Palace of Minos, the legendary King of the Minoans, a civilization that flourished well before the Trojan War, arising possibly as early as 3000 BC. Beginning in 1900 AD, Sir Arthur Evans excavated the site, and also, somewhat controversially, painted the place, adding decoration and restoring frescoes in the style of 1920s Art Deco. Mimi hustled me through the

Minoan site by a labyrinthine route that led to the most secluded corner of the ruins. Was this the cave of the Minotaur, the monstrous offspring of Pasiphaë, wife of Minos, half man, half bull, hidden away by the design of Daedalus? I scarcely had time to wonder before Mimi proceeded to dry-hump me. I liked Mimi, but I thought our relationship needed time to develop. Maybe I'd visit his tomato farm, or we'd at least have lunch together—maybe see a movie?—before we had sex. I tried to tell him that this was happening way too fast for me. The Greek for "fast" is *grígora*, and when Greeks want to emphasize something they say it twice, so I said, "*Grígora, grígora,*" meaning (I thought) "Too fast." It turns out that what I was saying was "Faster, faster."

Mimi did not teach me much about the Minoan civilization, but he did give me a glimpse into the prevailing view that a single woman traveling alone in the Mediterranean must be in want of a man. Except for a nice old guy with cataracts, the men all asked why I was traveling alone and refused to believe that I was alone by design. Where was my husband? Dining alone in restaurants, I was a tourist attraction unto myself. Eating is social, and the style of the Greeks is to share a lot of different dishes. If I wanted olives and tzatziki and calamari and what they called a χωριάτικη σαλάτα (*choriátiki*, or village, salad)— which didn't seem unreasonable—I was served enough to feed a family of four. The waiters, almost always men, flirted and asked personal questions and offered private tours of the Acropolis by motorbike. I could not sit down on a bench in public without being invited to a ménage à trois. I was not used to attracting so much sexual attention. While it flattered me, it also confused me. It would have been simpler to invent a husband—call him Menelaus—and explain that my old man was back at the hotel, or even let the Greek men come to the ego-salving conclusion that if I wasn't interested in them specifically, I must not like men in general.

I loved men, but I had a militant streak about making my way alone, and I was not to be derailed by a horny tomato farmer. The ultimate goal of my travels was Constantinople, or Konstantinoúpolis, as I insisted on calling it (Istanbul is a corruption of the Greek for *stin póli*, "to the city, in the city," understood to be the city of Constantine), and I wanted to reach it by way of Troy, the archaeological site near Çanakkale, in Turkey. I was on the trail of Homer. Because the *Iliad* and the *Odyssey* were written in the Ionic dialect of Greek, they are associated with the region around the island of Lesbos and the city of Smyrna on the mainland—Izmir in modern-day Turkey. Leaving Crete for the eastern Aegean, I made my way up the Dodecanese from Rhodes to Chios on boats that sailed under the blue and white stripes of the Greek flag, and then crossed over to the opposite coast on a boat that flew the flag of the Turks: red with a crescent moon and a star.

The closer I got to Turkey, the smaller the boat. The big ferries had full bars, with whiskey, beer, and wine, but that last boat, between Chios and Turkey, served only ouzo by the shot. I was sitting at the rail, nursing an ouzo in a small glass, stretching it with ice and water, and staring into the sea, when I suddenly understood the meaning of the Homeric epithet "wine-dark sea." The sea is blue, right? At least on a sunny day. Not purple like wine. Under clouds the sea is gray or greenish-gray. The Mediterranean may be turquoise along the edges, in the shallows, but out in the middle it is navy blue. There is a theory, perhaps inspired by the words "wine-dark," that the ancient Greeks didn't see the color blue, but I don't buy it. The Greeks lived in a world of blue. They had the open sea and the vault of the sky—maybe their eyes were so saturated with blue that they saw through it: it was transparent, like air. Blue was their enveloping medium, like water for fish. They had lapis, the most gorgeous of blue stones, and flax, which has a delicate powdery-blue flower. What came to me as I sipped my ouzo and gazed at the Aegean was that Homer wasn't saying that the sea was the *color* of wine. He was saying that the sea had the depths found in a cup of wine: that it was mysterious, hypnotic, dangerous. "Wine-dark" was a quality, not a color. It drew you in, you could lose yourself in it.

Çanakkale, the town closest to the site of ancient Troy, was a bit of a letdown. I had learned only three words of Turkish: water, bus, and thank you, and for thank you the Turks used *merci*. The default language for tourists was German. In an emergency, German would come back to me: *Es ist besser wenn ich nicht in dein Zimmer gehe.* It is better if I do not go to your room. In Çanakkale, I was taken under the wing of a man who had a small boy, and who answered all my questions with "Is possible." Anything was possible! It wasn't necessarily a good idea, but it was possible. He put me and all my luggage on a minibus to the ruins of Troy. The Turks had not mastered the tourist economy. There was no guard or guide or museum or brochure or ticket booth or Coke machine. There was a dusty lot with an incomprehensible plaque showing a series of strata in solid or dotted lines, dating the different settlements. The Turks had built a monumental wooden horse that served as a viewing platform, and which I mounted via wooden stairs. Troy was farther inland than I expected. Heinrich Schliemann, an amateur archaeologist from Germany, thought he had figured out from clues in Homer where the ancient city stood, and went there and dug. He dug right past Priam's Troy. That was in the 1870s, before the modern science and ethics of archaeology were in place, and Schliemann was careless by modern standards, and looted Troy.

It surprised me to learn that not everyone believes there really was a Trojan War. Of course there was a Trojan War! It was already ancient history when Homer and friends sang about it, having taken place hundreds of years earlier, around 1200 BC. To me, the proof that the Trojan War really happened is in the realistic touches in the *Iliad*. For instance, there are two characters named Ajax. Why would Homer give two characters the same name unless there really were two men named Ajax?

Fitzgerald calls them "Aías, tall and short." Another realistic touch is that one character goes by two names: Paris/Alexandros. He is mostly called Alexandros by the Greeks and the gods, and Paris by his family.

Traveling alone, without benefit of a local guide or a strong grasp of the language, had its frustrations, but they were in inverse proportion to the satisfaction I felt when I succeeded—when the ship came in and the anchor chain rattled down the hull and I trotted up the gangplank. The other tourists—couples and families and backpackers—would gather at the stern, waving goodbye to the place they'd just visited, while I was up at the prow, eager to move on to my next destination. The thrust of this journey was definitely forward.

ON THAT TRIP, I traced a spiral like a hurricane over the Aegean, through Constantinople—how cosmopolitan I felt, writing in my travel journal "Crossed the Dardanelles"—and overland to Thessaloniki, where I met up with some friends from New York, and we circled down to Delphi and the Peloponnese and back up to Athens. Even when something went wrong, it went right. Missing the ferry to Skiathos, in the Sporades (islands whose name implies that they were scattered in the sea), we spent a day driving around Mount Pelion and a night in Volos, the port of embarkation for Jason and his Argonauts in their search for the Golden Fleece (another big hit at the Lyceum). We bought cherries and sweet, tiny apricots from a woman who sold the fruit from her own trees, and who cut gardenias from her garden for us as parting gifts. Delphi, site of the oracle to Apollo, was full of liars and fake Greek spontaneity—boys who danced joylessly for tips at a tourist restaurant—but down the hill from Mount Parnassus, on the other side of the road, the guard at the sanctuary of Athena gave me a genuinely friendly greeting. His demesne, known as the Tholos, a round vaulted temple from the fourth century BC, was perfectly placed in the landscape: three reconstructed columns in gray and white banded marble, surmounted by a segment of the roof. He taught me to say *"stous Delphoús"* ("to Delphi")—the name of the city is plural, perhaps for its mythical inhabitants the dolphin people, and takes this form in the accusative—and gave me two chips of stone, the size of fingernails, that he picked up off the ground, one smooth and dark gray, the other ridged and pinkish like a shell: talismans.

On the way from Delphi down through the Peloponnese to the tourist destinations of Ancient Mycenae—the beehive tombs and cyclopean walls and the ancient, storied theater of Epidaurus—we got off the highway and onto the back roads. We had been catapulting over a landscape that we should have been rolling in, like bumblebees in hydrangea blossoms. The Peloponnese is Herakles country, full of places that evoke his name: Tiryns, where he was born; Nemea, where he slew the lion whose impenetrable skin he wore as a cape. Ours was the only car on the narrow road, with vineyards spread out on both sides. As we approached a crossroads, hoping for a sign—in both senses, cosmic and mundane: reassurance from the gods that we had made the right decision by getting off the highway, and an indication from the department of transportation that a right turn would take us to Nauplio— an oversized placard came into focus, pointing the way to . . . Ancient Cleones? Every time we reached an intersection, we were directed to Ancient Cleones. We were approaching Arcadia, the pastoral landscape of legend, and Hermes, the wayfarer, was messing with us.

The magic dissipated a bit in Nauplio, where we looked for a place to stay. A woman who ran a guest house—a devotee of Hera, I am guessing—refused to give me a room with a view, because it was a double and I was a single. I shouldn't have taken it personally. People need to make a living, and this was a matter of economics: you can put a single person in a double room, but you can't put a couple in a single room. By depriving me of the room with a view, and taking her chances that a nice juicy couple would come along (which they did), the landlady squeezed more money out of the tourist economy. I went off disgruntled into the streets of Nauplio while my friends headed for the sea, but I couldn't stay disgruntled for long. Here were purple-flowering trees such as I had never seen—jacarandas? The trumpet-shaped blossoms covered the trees and carpeted the path, as if it had been prepared for a procession. Later, looking at the wine list at dinner, we ordered a bottle of Nemean red—at the time, we pronounced it *Nee*-me-an, but I have since learned to say Ne-*may*-an—realizing that it was made from the grapes of the very vineyards we had driven through, with their bouquet of Herakles. That kept happening in Greece: the real world of crabby landladies and deceptive road signs would crack open and mythology would spill out. You have to pay the rent in the real world, but it's crazy not to embrace those moments when it intersects with eternity.

Instead of satisfying my wanderlust, that trip whetted my appetite for all things Greek. I came home determined to go back. Meanwhile, I would learn ancient Greek and tackle the classics. I was bent on reading Homer in the original. I wished there were some way I could *be* Greek, or at least pass for Greek, just by saturating myself in Greekness—the land, the sea, the language, the literature. Odysseus was a hero to me, and, like him, I wanted to have Athena on my side. She was, after all, the patron goddess of education. Maybe I could be Greek in spirit.

Of all the Olympians, Athena is the goddess whose attributes are hardest to define. If Odysseus is a man of many turnings, Athena is a master of disguise. She appears in many forms in Homer, from mentor—the old family friend, a precocious little girl, a tall, handsome woman outside the swineherd's gate—to swallow. She wears the aegis of her father—a goatskin trimmed with serpents—accessorized with the head of Medusa.

Although she is associated with war, she encourages diplomacy over warfare, intelligence over force, strategy over blunt attack, eternal vigilance over anarchy. She can terrify you and she can fill you with hope. She is both aggressor and protector. Athena expects a lot of us and brings out the best in us. She is certainly a friend to Odysseus, and maybe to all of us who are trying to get somewhere.

# CHAPTER 3

# DEAD OR ALIVE

◎◎

ANYONE WHO DOUBTS the value of studying a dead language should tune in to the Scripps National Spelling Bee, which is broadcast live on ESPN, like an Olympic event, with color commentary by lexicographers and up-close-and-personal interviews with the contestants. I thought I knew some Greek, but these elite athletes of orthography routinely spell Greek-derived words that I didn't even know existed, much less what they meant or how to spell them. The 2018 competition tapped a reservoir of Greek-derived words: ephyra, pareidolia, ooporphyrin, lochetic, ecchymosis, ochronosis, gnomonics (the art of making sundials), propylaeum (which means something like "foregate," as in the ceremonial entrance to the Acropolis of Athens). Pareidolia turns out to mean the all-too-human tendency to discern an image in some unexpected place, as "the face of the Virgin Mary on a toasted cheese sandwich," in the citation from *Webster's Unabridged*.

Ooporphyrin I figured had something to do with an egg (ᾠόν in ancient Greek) and purple (porphyry, the deep-red stone): a reference to some fabulous creature that lays purple eggs? Close. It is the characteristic pigment of brown eggshells.

The champion won on the word koinonia. This I had a bead on, because I knew that Koine was the word for biblical Greek. Koine means the common tongue, like lingua franca. So koinonia is the shared spirit in a community of believers. The bee pronouncer, Jacques Bailly, a former champion himself, offered alternative pronunciations of koinonia, one with the "oi" of classical Greek and the other with the "ee" of the modern language. Bailly won the bee in 1980, on the word elucubrate, from the Latin for "compose by lamplight," or study late into the night, burn the midnight oil. He is now a classics professor at the University of Vermont.

One boy progressed to the next round on Mnemosyne (Ne-*moz*-e-nee)—Memory, mother of the Muses, who gave us the mnemonic device. Mnemosyne ought to be the presiding deity of spelling bees. These kids had clearly burned some midnight oil as they trained in combining forms. There were a lot of polysyllabic German-derived words (Bewusstseinslage) in the bee, too, as well as impressionistic French words (cendre) that English has adopted. These borrowings bear the earmarks of their mother tongues: the German tendency to agglomerate, the French to nasalize. Like Bailly, the winner of the Scripps National Spelling Bee may build a career out of words.

The study of any language—Greek, Latin, Hebrew, German, French, Spanish, Portuguese, Japanese, Taino—opens the mind, gives you a window onto another culture, and reminds you that there is a larger world out there and different ways of saying things, hearing things, seeing things. It always distresses me to hear someone say, "I'm no good at foreign languages," or demand "English for me, dear." In learning a foreign language, you have to humble yourself, admit your ignorance, be willing to look stupid. We learn a language by making mistakes. Or anyway I do.

Spelling Greek-derived words in English is difficult enough, but spelling Greek words in Greek is like necromancy. And even though it is a phonetic language, pronunciation is problematic, because of the way stress hops around in Greek. In English, if you put the accent on the wrong syllable, people will usually understand you (though they may laugh at you, to your face or behind your back), but many Greek words are practically unrecognizable to Greeks if the stress is wrong, or they have a completely different meaning from the one you intended. I sometimes wonder what my beloved teacher Dorothy Gregory thought when she saw me off to Greece that first time. She didn't think it was a good idea to go at Easter, and it did make me feel alienated. Easter (Pascha) is a big family holiday, and I was a total stranger, a *xéni*. Dorothy would have cringed if she had heard me trying to keep up my end of the Easter greeting: "Christ is risen," a person says, and you are supposed to respond,

"Truly He is risen," but I got the ending on my adverb wrong and said, "Really? He is?"

Of course, no one in Greece expects an Irish-looking American to speak even a little bit of Greek. Most of them speak English so much better than I speak Greek that it's hard to find someone to practice on. At a farmers' market on Rhodes, I was excited to see artichokes for sale. "Αγκινάρες!" I said to the wizened old man at the vegetable stand (*agkináres*). In response, he said—in English—"Just tell me what you want." But as I was leaving with a couple of his long-stemmed beauties, I heard him say, in Greek, "How are they called in English?" I stopped, turned around, and said, "Arty choke." He repeated it: "Άρτι τσοκ." If I couldn't get them to teach me Greek, I would help them with their English.

In Piraeus once, investigating the marinas on the opposite side of the peninsula from the huge docks where the ferries come and go, I was invited by a restaurant owner to sit at a prime table, across the street from the restaurant's kitchen, overlooking the picturesque horseshoe-shaped harbor with yachts from all over the world. He started off in English, and I was feeling beaten down that day, so I ordered in English. After my meal, I crossed the street to use the WC, which was in the basement, and coming up the stairs I noticed a landing along the staircase that had been turned into a terrarium for tortoises. The Greek for tortoise is one of the words that has stuck with me, because I once heard a little boy, spotting a tortoise in the grass in Panorama, a suburb of Thessaloniki, shout "Χελώνα!" It was as if until that moment I did not really believe that Greeks called a tortoise a *chelóna*. Delighted by the tortoises, I counted them in Greek: *mía, dúo, treis, téssereis, pénte, éxi, eftá, októ—októ chelónes!* On my way out, I passed my waiter and said, in English, "You have eight tortoises!" "No!" he said, horrified. "We do not eat the tortoises!"

You're probably wondering if I ever get anything right.

In my first class I learned the Greek words for food and for numbers and for the seasons. The words for the seasons are especially beautiful in Greek. Spring is *ánoixi*, from the verb ανοίγω, open, uncork—the year opens. Summer is *kalokaíri*: literally, "good weather." *Phthinóporo* is the fall, suggestive of the last harvest and overripe fruit (the consonant cluster at the beginning, *phth*, at first seems rude to an English speaker, as if you were spitting out a cherry pit). Winter, *kheimónas,* is a time of storms and of scraping by.

From then on in, it's nouns and verbs, verbs and nouns. Nouns come first: naming things. Then verbs: going places and doing things. Soon enough you have to separate your verbs into tenses, and that's when it gets complicated and I move along to another language. In Spanish, I never got out of the present tense, forming the past by hooking my right thumb over my shoulder and the future by waving my left hand in front of me to indicate forward motion. I played the simpleton in Mexico, but I managed to eat and drink and buy Band-Aids.

My *New Yorker* boss Ed Stringham taught me the Greek for "yes" and "no," and we commiserated over the confusion that reigns between them. The German *ja* and *nein* have a clear resemblance to "yes" and "no." The French *oui* and the Italian *sì* and Spanish *sí* come easily enough, and all the Romance languages—even Portuguese—rely on the basic sound of "no": *no, non, não*. But the Greek for "yes" is *nai* (ναι), which sounds like "no" or "nah," a negative, while the word for "no" is όχι, which sounds like "OK," meaning "yes." Why must life be so cruel? Sometimes when I'm traveling I can't seem to get out the right word for "yes" in the country I'm in and I cycle through the whole litany: *Ja, oui, sì, nai*, yes. Όχι is fun to say, once you get used to it. A child sometimes draws out the first syllable—όοοχι, on a falling note—in protest. Greek Americans sometimes call October 28th, the day Greece entered the Second World War, Όχι Day, for the refusal by Metaxas, the prime minister, to let Mussolini's troops enter the country from Albania. Later, the Nazis would not take όχι for an answer.

Greeks often say "yes" twice—*"nai nai"*—like "yeah yeah," conveying an attitude, sometimes reassuring, sometimes impatient. The gesture that accompanies *nai*, equivalent to our nodding, is a single gracious tilt of the head, down and to the side. Όχι is accompanied by a sharp upward stab of the chin, which sometimes seems unnecessarily abrupt. At the newsstand, a taciturn newsagent will sometimes give you the chin flick to indicate that he is out of whatever you wanted. Sometimes he will add, "Feenees," meaning "Finished" or "All gone."

The Greeks also have their own way of saying "OK": *entáxei* (εντάξει), which means, literally, "in order" and brings us back to the classroom. Τάξη (the nominative in modern Greek) means "class," as in classroom, where one expects order and discipline. The tricky thing here is to remember that although the stress is on the alpha in εντάξει, when you want a taxi you have to put the stress on the last syllable: ταξί. Otherwise, you are standing on a street corner like an idiot calling out "Class, class!" or "Order, order!" How is anyone supposed to know you want a cab?

Because I could not go back to infancy and learn Greek from the cradle, I made the best of it: I used English to help me learn Greek. There is a lot of Greek in English. Like those first words I learned in order to be polite, *parakaló* and *efkharistó*, other words stuck with me because of their echoes in English. When I arrived at the Hotel Achilleus in Athens, and the receptionist pointed me toward the elevator—one of those tiny European hoisting cages that make you think too much about weights and pulleys—I tried out my Greek, asking "Λειτουργεί;" (*Leitourgeí?*) "Does it work?" (The question mark in Greek looks like a semicolon.) This word had stuck because of its connection with "liturgy": the rituals and prayers that are the work of the Church. The receptionist, who moved easily from Greek to German, English, and French, said *nai*—of course the elevator worked. I found it a little rickety and had the urge to pray when I was in it.

Dorothy Gregory gave me a lot of vocabulary—I have a box of Greek, some of it in her handwriting—but the words that stuck are the ones she used conversationally, in direct address, bringing the word out of the dictionary and into the moment, like the time she said, "Διψάς;" (*Dipsás?*), and I understood that she was asking, "Are you thirsty?" I knew that a dipsomaniac was someone with an insatiable thirst, but to hear Dorothy use the verb διψάω in the second-person singular present tense and to match it with my parched throat was a revelation. Ναι, διψάω. What are we going to do about it? Is there a water fountain out in the hallway? I wonder if this is why I feel moved whenever I see a Greek man watering a plant or setting out a bowl of water for a dog. To give someone water is to care.

ALL THESE WORDS are modern Greek, which is very much alive. When the English-speaking world needs to name something, it turns to the ancient language. Many words from the natural world come from Greek: ocean, dolphin, hippopotamus, peony, elephant, pygmy. Some of the words that come from ancient Greek (and survive in modern Greek) are for exotic creatures. Octopus is from the Greek: οκτώ (eight) + πους (foot) = eight-legger. (Having learned of its intelligence, I no longer order grilled octopus in restaurants.) Like the octopus, the medusa, or jellyfish, is one of the original sea monsters. So is the hippocampus, or seahorse. The elephant may go back to our old friend the Phoenician aleph, ox.

Some words that look as if they came directly from the

Greek turn out, on further study, to have followed a more circuitous route. For instance, the eucalyptus—ευ (good, well) + καλυπτος (covered) = well-covered, as in a hooded blossom—is native to Australia; the word's first recorded use was in 1788 AD. Of course, it's also ευκάλυπτος in modern Greek, from English, through ancient Greek. In the Peloponnese once, when somebody identified a fragrant tree that looked to me like wild white wisteria as ακακία, acacia, I wondered briefly if the Greek ακακία was a transliteration of the English. Which came first, the word or the tree? The thorny acacia is native to Africa and the Middle East, not a transplant from the New World, so ακακία came before acacia, but the tree itself no doubt preceded the word.

The names for natural phenomena, like flowers and insects, are often local. For instance, when I was a child, our word for the gnats or midges that swarmed all over Cleveland on muggy summer nights was Canadian soldiers. I picked this up with no idea that it might be interpreted as a slur against our neighbors on the opposite shore of Lake Erie—I just thought it was the bugs' name. My grandmother used to decorate the narrow strip of land between the house and the driveway with a nasty, shrubby little plant called live-forever. I didn't like it as a child and I don't like it now, though I allowed a friend to plant some in my garden under the name sedum. It is a dull plant, though I must admit that its common name is highly descriptive: it does seem to live forever.

Some Greek flower names are actually pre-Greek: they

derive ultimately from people and languages that predated ancient Greek. For instance, narcissus (*nárkissos*) was the original Greek word for the flower, native to southern Europe, we commonly call the daffodil. The myth of Narcissus, the beautiful youth who fell in love with his own reflection, is the timeless personification of the flower, accounting for its existence. The word narcissus is related to the Greek *nárke*, or torpor, numbness, a narcotic quality. Daffodil seems to be a corruption of the Greek asphodel, the flower of Hades and the dead. Jonquil is a Frenchier name for a species of the same flower. The hyacinth is another flower with a myth attached: Hyacinthus was a Greek youth beloved of Apollo who was accidentally killed by the god, who then turned him into a flower.

Greek actually has two words for flower, the ancient *ánthos* and the frivolous modern *louloúdi*. For *The Greek Anthology*, a collection of the best work of the Greek lyric poets, poems were selected as if they were flowers: a word bouquet.

George Orwell lamented the tendency to overlay classical names on common English flowers. He writes that "a snapdragon is now called an antirrhinum, a word no one can spell"—much less pronounce—"without consulting a dictionary," and that "forget-me-nots are coming more and more to be called myosotis." Orwell adds, "I don't think it a good augury for the future of the English language that 'marigold' should be dropped in favour of 'calendula.'" I agree that something is lost when pinks are called "dianthus" and foxglove gives way to "digitalis." The point is that flowers bloomed before people had books to look up their names in, and in the places where the flowers bloom, people tend to have their own names for them.

It is mainly words for things that were imported to Greece in modern times that have been transliterated into Greek from other languages. For instance, the Greeks did not have beer worth mentioning until the great powers of Europe installed Otto von Wittelsbach, of Bavaria, as their king, in 1832, and he brought along a brewer. The Greeks drafted their word for beer, μπίρα, from the Italian *birra*.

Many medical words are from the Greek, possibly because much of what we think of as medicine began in Greece. Physicians take the Hippocratic Oath, named for Hippocrates, but the notion that it begins with "First, do no harm" is a myth. Hippocrates is generally regarded as the first to treat illness as a natural phenomenon rather than a punishment from the gods. The symbol of the caduceus on the back of an ambulance—a staff with two snakes wound around it—is derived from Greek mythology: it resembles the Rod of Asclepius, the healer and son of Apollo, which has a single snake climbing up it. Greeks gave entirely too much credit to snakes, in my opinion. But I suppose they're better than leeches.

For a long time, I went around thinking that words like otorhinolaryngologist (ear, nose, and throat doctor, diminished in English to ENT), ophthalmologist, and orthodontist were of Greek origin, and they are, but not in the sense that ancient Greeks consulted such specialists or wore metal braces on their teeth. Demosthenes the orator did not consult a speech therapist; legend has it that he filled his mouth with pebbles and addressed the sea, so that when he removed the pebbles and spoke to an audience his voice was clear and powerful. Those English words were put together from Greek parts—little linguistic Frankenstein's monsters—as the specialties came into being.

An educated medical professional in Victorian times probably studied Latin and Greek, though not all doctors were classicists. Still, when it came time to name things, they fell back on Greek, possibly because it was the oldest, most stable, most dignified source. There might have been a mystification factor: fancy words impress people. Old English had its own words for body parts: lungs, blood, kidney, gut, elbow, knee. We don't need the Greek words, but the language is the richer for them: we have two ways of saying the same thing. Perhaps the Greek words create a comforting distance between us and our bodies. Would you rather have tennis elbow or epicondylitis? Water on the brain or hydrocephalus? A doctor might call someone a hemophiliac where a mother would bemoan a bleeder. The Greek terms ennoble the ailment, even if they don't make it go away. Liver disease is hepatitis. Nephritis afflicts the kidneys. Arthritis—what my mother used to call Arthuritis—refers to the joints and is somehow more abstract than joint disease (though I'd rather not have either).

Greek casts a spell of importance over the body parts and the doctors, a spell that a physician might be tempted to exploit. I had some green spots on my toes one summer—I'd been spending a lot of time barefoot on the beach—and I asked my doctor about them. "That's just pigment," he said. All he did, in his diagnosis, was use the fancy word for color. If surgeons knew that the word surgery comes from the ancient Greek *cheirourgía*—χειρ (hand) + έργον (work)—meaning "handiwork" and could apply as well to needlepoint as to brain surgery, they might not be so arrogant.

We are all still humans, in pursuit of the same dreams that inspired our remotest ancestors. Igor Sikorsky, the father of the modern helicopter, built on the work of Daedalus, the original inventor, who made wings out of feathers and wax, which he and his son, Icarus, used to escape Crete. Everyone knows what happened: Icarus flew too close to the sun, the wax melted, and he dropped into what is now called the Icarian Sea. The word helicopter combines helix (spiral) and *pteryx* (wing, as in pterodactyl, the prehistoric bird with leathery-looking finger wings). In plain English, we call it a chopper.

Or take the telephone, patented by Alexander Graham Bell. It makes use of the Greek stems for distance (τηλε) and voice (φωνη): voice from afar. The Irish word for telephone is *guthán* (*goo*hawn), loosely translated as "voice box," made by adding a suffix to the Irish word for voice. In English, we sometimes refer to the telephone as the horn ("Get him on the horn!"), but the inventor wanted a new word for his revolutionary invention, and "telephone" stuck. Why do we lean on dead languages for new things? Perhaps expressing these things in the language that is oldest, in words that we have in common with many other languages, gives us a touchstone.

THE AUTHORITATIVE SOURCE on ancient Greek words is Liddell and Scott's Greek-English Lexicon, first published in 1843. (Some classicists pronounce the name Lid*dell*.) Its origins are somewhat mythical: in one version, a publisher approached a student named Robert Scott with the idea for a Greek-English lexicon, and Scott said he would do it only if his friend Henry George Liddell would share the work.

Liddell was said to be the epitome of an Oxford don. Tall, white-haired, and aristocratic, he was ordained in the Church of England and was chaplain to Prince Albert, the husband of Queen Victoria. He and his wife had ten children, one of whom was to become "the most famous little girl in English literature": Alice Liddell. Charles Lutwidge Dodgson used to watch her and her sisters playing in the deanery garden as he worked in the library. She inspired him, as Lewis Carroll, to write the stories that turned into *Alice's Adventures in Wonderland* and *Through the Looking-Glass*. An early adopter of the camera, Dodgson photographed Alice in different costumes and poses. These days, he would be summoned before a committee on sexual misconduct. Alice was also pursued by John Ruskin, but, unimpressed with her literary suitors, she married a cricketer named Reginald Hargreaves.

Liddell and Scott began work in 1834, basically translating a Greek-German lexicon by one Franz Passow, who in turn had based his work on a dictionary begun by Johan Gotlob Schneider earlier that century.

To classicists, a lexicon differs from a dictionary in being a collection of words occurring in the work of a given group of authors, with citations and definitions. Passow had begun with Homer and Hesiod and started on Herodotus; Liddell and Scott picked up with Herodotus and Thucydides. Liddell's biographer describes their method: "The uses of each word were traced from its simplest and most rudimentary meaning to its various derivative and metaphorical applications. . . . [E]ach gradation was illustrated as far as possible historically, by apt quotations from authors of successive dates."

Scott's career took him to Cornwall, where he was not well situated to continue work on the lexicon. (No email.) Liddell became dean of Christ Church, Oxford. In July 1842, he wrote to Scott, "You will be glad to hear that I have all but finished Π"—pi— "that two-legged monster, who must in ancient times have worn his legs a-straddle, else he could never have strode over so enormous a space as he has occupied and will occupy in Lexicons." By the time Liddell published the eighth edition, in 1897, fifty-four years later—a year before his death—the volume included vocabulary from the dramatists and philosophers. It was later enlarged by Henry Stuart Jones, and the 1968 edition, with supplement, runs to more than 2,000 pages.

Before Liddell and Scott, the only way for an English speaker to learn Greek was through Latin. As Liddell and Scott wrote in a preface to the lexicon, they intended the work to "foster and keep alive . . . that tongue which, as the organ of Poetry and Oratory, is full of living force and fire, abounding in grace and sweetness, rich to overflowing . . . that tongue in which some of the noblest works of man's genius lie enshrined—works which may be seen reflected faintly in imitations and translations, but of which none can know the perfect beauty, but he who can read the words themselves, as well as their interpretation."

ONE OF THE THINGS that make a language a language, that give it currency, is the small, indefinable, not strictly necessary words that connect you to the person you're talking to. They might be slang, they might be idiom, they might be baby talk. Linguists dryly call them "function words"; in Greek grammar they are known as particles. They rope you in. In English we use them all the time and are almost helpless not to use them. If we become self-conscious about them, we are tongue-tied. Some people deplore the extra words as loose and repetitive, and complain that kids today are lazy and inarticulate and that they are destroying the beauty and precision of the language. But we have relied on such little words since antiquity. They enrich the language as they help us get along with one another.

I overheard a young woman on the street say to her companion, "And then I like flipped out last week actually?" What was she saying, with those extra words and the interrogatory intonation? Stripped to its essentials, her sentence would be "I flipped out last week." The conjunction "and," the adverb "then," the ubiquitous all-purpose "like," and the intensifier "actually" combine to smooth out the utterance, tuck it into a larger story, and appeal for understanding. The question mark, for upspeak, lends piquancy, as if to substitute for "you know?" at the end and signal that the woman is not finished, that there were consequences to her flipping out.

English is loaded with particles, words and expressions that float up constantly in speech: like, totally, so, you know, OK, really, actually, honestly, literally, in fact, at least, I mean, quite, of course, after all, hey, fuck, sure enough . . . know what I mean? Just sayin'. And it's not only the young who use them. Some particles function as sentence adverbs: hopefully, surely, certainly. Some are conjunctions with attitude ("and furthermore . . ."), conjuring a shaken fist. They keep the conversation going. Although they have no content, they are the soul of the language.

Particles are used to ingratiate, to engage. I once heard myself say in the locker room at the pool, "Is there like no hot water?" To someone my own age or older, I might have said, "Isn't there any hot water?" But I was speaking to a younger person. My choice of words was not conscious manipulation; I was making a spontaneous effort to blend in (difficult at a public pool). Similarly, in conversation, I might say, "So, you know, I was like totally blown away," but in writing I might edit it to the more contained "I was impressed."

Writing has its own fillers—"as it were," "as one does," "be that as it may," "without further ado"—some of them more formal and stilted than others. Orin Hargraves, in *It's Been Said Before: A Guide to the Use and Abuse of Clichés*, tracks the frequency with which writers (especially journalists) use such phrases, which are perhaps better described as idioms than clichés but are nonetheless formulaic. As a copy editor, I have often been tempted to strip them out. "Truth be told," as a transition, is way overused.

Particles define the speech patterns of friends, especially when they are poets or writers with idiosyncratic language habits, overwhelmed with the need for self-expression. A poet friend often stammers "and and and," until I want to scream, "Spit it out!" Another friend is partial to the construction "didn't I just," as in "Didn't I just leave my phone on the park bench." This has a slightly self-deprecatory tang, as if to comment on typical self-sabotaging behavior. There are people who bob their heads up and down while they're talking to you or offer significant eyebrow action, which is intended to get you to agree with them. (Resist!) "Yada yada yada" is another version of the poet's "and and and." A friend used to pronounce it "Ya*da* ya*da* ya*da*." Some of these speech patterns are lovable. I think of William F. Buckley, Jr., stammering and flicking his tongue in a debate, or David Foster Wallace repeatedly using "And but so" to great effect, like a trademark, in his essays.

And how did we ever get along without OK? OK is a pivot point (OK, now I'm going to write about OK); it elicits a response from the listener (I'm going to talk about OK, OK?); it announces the beginning of the end of the discussion (So that's all I have to say, OK?). OK has become such a feature of informal speech that we play with it, texting the single letter K, or affecting an Australian accent, Kye?

English has a sack load of these sometimes charming, often indefinable turns of phrase, and guess what: so does ancient Greek. It is because of the particles in Plato that Socrates has such a warm presence. Particles give personality to his language. Without them, it might be an automaton speaking. I was amazed, in reading Plato's *Apology of Socrates*, how much nuance these syllables give to Socrates' speech—they act like nudges, winks, facial expressions. You can almost see Socrates poking his listener as you hear his confidential "don't ya know," a folksy expression from a sage older generation. Herbert Weir Smyth, of Harvard University, devoted 40 pages of his 1920 *Greek Grammar* to particles. Another scholar, J. D. Denniston, published a 600-page book titled *The Greek Particles*, devoted solely to the subject, in

1934. Smyth (whose name rhymes with "writhe") writes that particles "often resist translation by separate words, which in English are frequently over emphatic and cumbersome in comparison to the light and delicate nature of the Greek originals."

One of the first particles a student of ancient Greek learns comes in a pair: μέν and δέ. They are traditionally translated as "on the one hand . . . and on the other hand . . ." In English, this has always seemed to me, on the one hand, heavy-handed, predictable, and boring. On the other hand, there is no denying that it works as a rhetorical device. At *The New Yorker*, someone could not write "on the other hand" if he had not already written "on the one hand," or we'd point that out. Greek was not so stern. People fall in love with μέν and δέ, swooning over the way their habitual use demonstrates something about the Greek character, as if the notion of antithesis were baked right into the language.

One of the simplest particles, still in use in modern Greek, is καί, a conjunction meaning "and" and an adverb meaning "even, also, too." When the Greeks rolled out a list—a series—they would repeat καί between the items, and this repetitive "and" would have no more weight than a comma. They never had to think about the serial comma. Καί εγώ is translated as a modest demurral, "I on my part"; colloquially, we might be tempted to render it IMHO. Καί has also been translated as "pray," to stress the word that follows, as in "Pray, *you* try to explain particles." In combination with other particles, καί "often has an emphasis which is difficult to render,"

Smyth writes. Τι καί (literally "what and") can mean, in polite terms, "What on earth?" or, in saltier terms, "What the fuck?"

WTF, Socrates?

Unfortunately, as Smyth says, these untranslatable verbal inflections often get translated anyway, laboriously or to antiquated effect. Shakespeare can get away with "forsooth" and "methinks," but Socrates was not an Elizabethan. Jesus says, "Verily I say unto you," but Socrates was not a New Testament figure, either. He was a real person who said the sorts of thing a Jewish grandmother might say, like "Alright already."

So what are we supposed to do? On the one hand, a stiff translation will not gain Socrates any followers, and, on the other hand, an informal approach can sound glib. Rossellini, in his film *Socrates*, has Socrates part with his followers by saying *"A presto"*—"See you soon." Smyth specifies one use of μέν δή, which is slightly different from δέ, in an expression that he translates as "So much for that," an idiom that the translator Robert Fitzgerald puts into the mouth of Odysseus when he has finished off Penelope's suitors. This made me burst out laughing, but apparently it is exactly the sort of thing the Greeks said to one another when they wrapped something up.

As a copy editor, accustomed to pointing out clichés and repetitions and, you know, extra verbiage (writers still sometimes get paid by the word), I am alert to and often averse to space fillers in written English, though I am aware that these things serve a purpose. If I were Plato's copy editor, would I edit all the juice out of Socrates? There are things in Greek that are more delicate than anything in English, and the particles are the connective tissue not just in conversation but in formal prose and poetry. For instance, the librarians of Alexandria could, with the flick of a pen, distinguish the particle νῦν, with a circumflex accent, meaning "now, as the case stands, as it is," from νυν, meaning "now" in the inferential sense, marking, as Smyth ably puts it, "the connection of the speaker's thought with the situation in which he is placed." At *The New Yorker*, we had our own solution for differentiating the force of "now": in the temporal sense, meaning "at this moment" ("Now is the time for all good men to come to the aid of the party," the line that ancient typists traditionally used to test a typewriter), "now" stands alone, but in the rhetorical, stylistic sense ("Now, you're not going to like this") we would set "now" off with a comma, a cue of punctuation intended to bring the reader along with ease.

Smyth attributes another such subtle effect to a particle he calls the "untranslatable τέ." This is a connective—a conjunction like "and"—that introduces a clause and "has the effect of showing that its clause corresponds in some way to the preceding clause." Oh my God, it's a semicolon! Perhaps this is why ancient Greek didn't have a lot of punctuation—it didn't need it. The punctuation was built in.

Among classicists, of course, ancient Greek is far from dead. It is alive and wide open to interpretation, an object of fascinated speculation. One of the things I most love about Homer lives on as a source of endless controversy among classicists: his use of epithets. That there is still so much to be said about the Homeric epithet, a poetic device that is supposedly frozen in time, like the 5,000-year-old mummy found in the Alps, seems to me proof that ancient Greek is alive and well. Individual epithets continue to be reinterpreted and to inspire fresh translations. How can something that keeps unfolding possibly be dead?

In modern Greek, *epthetos* simply means "adjective," but Homeric epithets are loaded. An epithet, in its simplest form, identifies a character, endows him with individuality. For instance, I might refer to "my garrulous mother" or "her with the gift of gab." Homer might be the source for the advice given to aspiring fiction writers: label a character with a defining feature or bit of business and reinforce it now and then to remind the reader. "Crooked-minded Kronos" never lets us forget the harsh nature of this god.

In the *Iliad*, nearly every minor character has some distinctive feature, especially at the moment of death. Epithets of the major characters conjure some personal quality, often thrillingly ambiguous, and that quality often acts as a catalyst for drama. Achilles is invariably "swift-footed," and the reminders of this trait increase the terror of the scene in which he chases Hector around the citadel of Troy. *Polytropos*, the epithet most often given to Odysseus, contains the word for many and the word for turn and has been translated in countless ways, everything from ingenious and resourceful to wily and manipulative. The epithet both inspires and eludes translators and gives Odysseus a mercurial character, which colors his adventures and suggests that our hero may have been something of a sneak.

But the epithets are not always distinctive. In search of Homer, the classics scholar Milman Parry studied oral poetry in Yugoslavia in the 1930s. Building on his dissertation of 1928, he formed the radical conclusion that epithets, which come in different metrical lengths, were largely a device that oral poets relied on to fill out a line or give them time to think of what came next. In other words, Homer vamped. Epic poetry was an oral tradition, and as such it relied on repetition. The rhapsodes and their audiences were illiterate. They had no sense that there was anything wrong with being repetitive.

Our culture is a written one. We document everything. We like variety; repetition bores us. So do we have any use for the same Homeric tricks? Translators, depending on their bent, faithfully follow Homer by using the epithets whenever he does (Richmond Lattimore), deploy the epithets judiciously (Robert

Fitzgerald), vary them for the modern reader (Emily Wilson), crack them wide open (Christopher Logue), or do without (Stephen Mitchell).

But repetition has its uses. Before the invention of writing, it was the only way to remember things. In the *Odyssey*, the rams and ewes of the Cyclops are repeatedly described as fat and fleecy, and the Cyclops' routine of bringing them in at night and milking the ewes in rigid order begins to seem a little labored: OK, Homer, we get it—Polyphemus may have his flaws, but he is good with animals and his system for cheesemaking cannot be beat. But then it turns out that whether or not he brings the rams inside along with the ewes is crucial, because Odysseus uses those rams, which need to be fat and fleecy, tied in threes, to make his escape, slinging his men under them (and saving the biggest ram for himself), so that in the morning the Cyclops, blind now, will not feel the stowaways as he pats down his livestock on their way out. The repetition is like theme music that builds suspense.

"Gray-eyed Athena" is one of Homer's most famous epithets, and something that drew me to Athena from the beginning. I have my mother's gray eyes (but not her gift of gab), so it pleased me to think I had something in common with Athena. Homer doesn't describe just anyone's eyes. Hera is "ox-eyed," meaning, I suppose, that her eyes are wide set and a deep liquid brown, with a suggestion of strength and stubbornness. If Athena's eyes are so important, the epithet "gray-eyed" must convey something ineffable about her character.

The word that Homer relies on for Athena is *glaukópis* (γλαυκῶπις), with that *op* familiar from "optic"—of the eye— and even from Cyclo*p*es, and *glaukós* carrying a range of meanings, one of them traditionally "gray." He also uses *glaukós* to describe the sea—I picture gray-green—but, like "wine-dark" (*oinóps*), *glaukópis* may refer to a quality instead of a color. In this case, it would mean not the sea's profound depths but its glittering surface. Gray-eyed is the traditional translation of *glaukópis*, used by both Lattimore and Fitzgerald. The variant spellings—gray (American) and grey (British)—shouldn't make any difference, but they do. I know a copy editor who refused to change "grey" to "gray" in a poem, per *New Yorker* style, because he insisted there was a difference. (He was also a poet.) Grey, with the "ey," suggests the spelling of "eye," perhaps giving it more luster. The original Loeb translation, "flashing-eyed Athena," comes with a footnote acknowledging the translation "grey-eyed," but adding "if colour is meant it is almost certainly blue."

We think of Greeks as having olive complexions and dark eyes, like Latinos, but some of the ancestors of the ancient Hellenes originally came from the north, and even today you often meet Greeks who have startling pale-blue eyes, as if lit from within by the Mediterranean. There are surely as many shades of blue as there are of gray/grey: cornflower, sapphire, royal, navy, aquamarine, cobalt, cerulean, indigo, Wedgwood, powder, metallic, cendre. There is Delft blue, the blue of chicory blooming wild along the interstate, the heavenly blue of the morning glory, hyacinth and hydrangea blue, robin's-egg blue, the ravishing blue of the Tasmanian superb fairy wren. There is Alice blue, swimming-pool blue, and gas-jet blue, and the dusty blue of blueberries. And don't forget forget-me-not blue. The blue of Windex, the primary blue of Marge Simpson's hair. There is the memorable blue of my father's eyes, the true blue of my younger brother's eyes tearing up on a morning of *acqua alta* in Venice. My older brother has clear blue eyes with more gray in them. People sometimes insist that I have blue eyes, but it isn't so. My eyes, like my mother's, are gray with a yellow ring around the pupil that shades into green, depending on the light. When I'm angry or when I've been crying and my eyes are red-rimmed, they are indisputably green. I would gladly step up to the epithet of Athena, but the form for a driver's license does not have a box to check for the eye color "glaucous."

Translators have tried all kinds of variants to give Athena's eyes something that gets at her character. Caroline Alexander, the first woman to translate the entire *Iliad* into English, initially used "gray-eyed" as the epithet for Athena, concurring with Lattimore, but, on looking further into it, she changed her translation to "gleaming-eyed." Searching Liddell and Scott, Alexander told me, she found an instance in which a verb related to the adjective *glaukópis* was used, by Homer, to describe a lion's eyes; eyes can shine, but they cannot gray (only hair does that). Besides, the big cats have green or amber eyes. Alexander thinks of Athena's eyes, evocatively, as "the color of wet stones."

For an entry in *The Homer Encyclopedia*, the classical scholar Laura Slatkin suggests "silvery-eyed." Robert Fagles goes with "bright-eyed goddess," which suggests enthusiasm. Christopher Logue, the master of anachronisms, experiments with "the prussic glare," which sounds alchemical, and "ash-eyed," which has a matte quality, as well as "Ringsight-eyed," which might refer to the eyes of the owl. Pausanias, a Greek who documented his extensive travels during the early Roman era (mid-second century AD; he is often called the Baedeker of ancient Greece), describes an image of Athena near the Temple of Hephaestus in Athens as having gray-green eyes, in the translation of Peter Levi; in one version of the myth, she is the daughter of Poseidon and therefore has eyes the color of the sea. Levi notes the connection to "owl-eyed"—the word *glaukós* is similar to *glaux*, the ancient Greek for "owl"—suggesting that Athena sees in the dark. Watchful Athena.

The various editions of Liddell and Scott provide several definitions for γλαυκός, some of them to do with quality and others with color. In the Little Liddell, as the abridged version is called, the definitions begin with "gleaming, glancing, bright-gleaming" and go on to "pale green, bluish green, gray." Liddell and Scott specifies that when eye color is meant the word means "light blue or gray," adding that in Latin *glaucus* means "of the olive, of the willow, and also of the vine" (perhaps olive green is the color of the silvery leaves, not the appetizers stuffed with red pimientos). The epithet of Minerva, Athena's Roman counterpart, is translated "with gleaming eyes." But Lewis and Short, the Latin equivalent of Liddell and Scott, defines *glaucus* as "bright, sparkling, gleaming, grayish." So gray-eyed Athena dates from the days when Greek was filtered through Latin.

I asked my Greek teacher, Chrysanthe, what γλαυκός means in modern Greek. She did not hesitate for long before replying, "Pale blue." If you pursue blue (*galázios*) in a modern Greek dictionary, it expands into sea green and azure, the particular blue of the sky. *Webster's* defines azure as the "blue color of the clear sky." It's hard to get away from the sky when you are talking about blue. The Greek *galaxías* (galaxy) means the Milky Way, a reference as much to the tinge of blue in milk as to the swath of white in the midnight sky.

Turning to the big American dictionary, *Webster's Second Unabridged*, I found *glauco-* as a combining form meaning silvery, gray (like the leaves of the olive tree?). Glaucoma is traced to the Greek for light gray, blue gray (like cloudy eyes?). For the mineral glauconite, the Greek root is defined as bluish-green or gray; glaucous is "of green-blue hue" and "yellowish green." Merriam-Webster's unabridged online dictionary really has room to spread out. For color, under glaucous, it offers pale yellow, green, and light bluish gray or bluish white. Latin *glaucus* and Greek *glaukós* may be related to an Old English word meaning pure, clear. So the color associated with *glaukópis* has evolved, changing with the circumstances, the way eyes change color depending on what a person is wearing or her mood. *Webster's Unabridged Online* goes on to offer separate, detailed definitions for shades of glaucous blue, glaucous gray, and glaucous green.

Surely Homer meant for Athena's eyes to be beautiful—a poet would not dwell on the description of a goddess's eyes to say they were as two thumbholes poked in a blackberry pie. These eyes are intelligent. They show purpose, they are expressive, they are sometimes complicit, conspiratorial. Emily Wilson, in her translation of the *Odyssey*, ransacked the thesaurus for Athena: she gives her "twinkling eyes," "glowing eyes," "shining eyes," "glinting eyes," "sparkling eyes." The goddess is "clear-eyed," "owl-eyed," "bright-eyed," "sharp-sighted." Her eyes are "aglow," "steely." At one point, Wilson even has her wink. Athena looks mortals in the eye. She levels with them through her gaze. Maybe, like the rosy fingers of dawn and the wine-dark sea, the gray-eyed goddess is so called not because of what her eyes look like but because of their effect on whomever she is looking at. Whatever color these eyes are—I would go with pale-green bluish-green gray—they are engaging.

That all this speculation on shades of gray and blue and green and yellow and silver, with qualities as various as the moods of the sky and the sea, springs from a single ancient compound adjective, γλαυκῶπις, describing a goddess who has our welfare at heart, seems to me proof of the vitality of words, their adaptability and strength and resilience. Good words never die. They keep on growing.

# CHAPTER 4

# DEMETER DEAREST

⊘⊘

WHEN I LEFT CLEVELAND for college in 1970, I was as a sealed bottle of milk: wholesome and protected from experience. When anyone asked where I was from, I'd say the Midwest. If they inquired further, I'd say Ohio. And if they still weren't satisfied I'd admit I was from Cleveland. The West Side. Near the zoo. Cleveland was a joke—it was the place where the river caught on fire. The DJs there called it "the best location in the nation." We called it "the mistake on the lake."

I had gone to an all-girls Catholic high school. By the time I was eighteen, I had traveled as far west as Detroit, as far south as Columbus, and as far east as Niagara Falls. The lake—Lake Erie—was north. I dreamed of going to boarding school in Switzerland and learning to speak French, German, and Italian. Radcliffe, Smith, and Wellesley were the stuff of fantasy. My father could afford to send me to a state university in Ohio. And he wanted to keep me in Ohio. I was determined to get out.

My senior year in high school, a friend who was researching colleges told me, "You should go to Rutgers—it has a renowned department of dairy science." I had a thing about cows. Placid, motherly creatures, cows evoked for me the pastoral life, and my affection for them extended to all aspects of the dairy industry— barns, silos, milk, cheese, cow paintings. Eventually, I drove a milk truck in Cleveland—the best job I've ever had. (Packaging mozzarella at a cheese factory in Vermont was the worst job I ever had. Copy editing at *The New Yorker* was the longest job I ever had.) As a teenager, I dreamed of having three cows and a bull on a dairy farm somewhere green and pristine, preferably Vermont, and initially I pursued that dream as far as the Garden State.

Rutgers, for all its Ivy League–sounding name, is a state university—*The* State University of New Jersey—and the tuition was only $200 more a semester than the tuition at an Ohio state university, an amount that I could earn at my after-school job. (I was a price marker in the clothing department of a discount store called Uncle Bill's.) So I applied to Douglass, the women's college of Rutgers University.

My father relented, and in the fall of 1970 we headed east on the Pennsylvania Turnpike. We made it as far as Norristown and spent the night in King of Prussia—these names delighted me—and in the morning we headed up the New Jersey Turnpike to New Brunswick. After delivering me to the dorm, my father gripped me by the shoulders, gave me a quick kiss, and said, "I don't like long goodbyes." He kept his head tilted back to hold the tears in. I was sad, too, but this was a turning point: I'd made it happen and I had no regrets.

On George Street was Dave's Food Store—a straightforward-enough name for a grocery store—and a ramshackle house with something purple blooming on the porch. It was the color of lilacs, but lilacs bloom only in the spring. What an enchanted, alien place I had landed in! The purple flower turned out to be wisteria, which keeps on blooming if you prune it. I have since inhaled it on Capri and Corfu and eaten it on Martha's Vineyard and planted a vine of my own in Rockaway, where it is eating my bungalow.

But the punch line of my escape from Ohio is that many of the New Jersey natives at Douglass had friends who had gone in the opposite direction: "Ohio is full of good schools," they said—Oberlin, Hiram, Case Western Reserve. "Why did you come here?"

New Jersey had the ocean, for one thing. I had never seen the ocean. I didn't know much else about the state—I thought its capital was Atlantic City. A new friend, appalled that I had never seen the ocean, borrowed a car and drove me to Asbury Park. I remember the thrill of being on the boardwalk and knowing instinctively that the ocean was to the east. In Cleveland, the water was always north. My orientation to the whole continent changed!

My first English class at Douglass was Autobiography, and we started with Sylvia Plath: *The Colossus* and *Ariel*. Her suicide angered me. I felt that as a college freshman I was being introduced to something ugly, to despair. Here was a published poet, a woman who had gone to Smith and married a handsome British poet and had children—she had everything—who seemed never to have recovered from her father's death, and somehow, reading her poetry, I felt as if I had to entertain her death wish. The other book that had a profound effect on me was Mary McCarthy's *Memories of a Catholic Girlhood*. She wrote about her defiance, as a girl, toward the idea that there *must* be a God because someone—something—had to have existed in order to create the universe: wasn't it just as easy to believe that the universe existed all along? (There is probably a name for this brand of heresy.) I was appalled at some of the things Mary McCarthy wrote. OK, so she didn't believe in God—did she have to insult him? I would have hedged my bets. I expressed this in class, and when the professor said that he was an atheist himself I was horrified. I already liked this man, but I was Catholic—how could I like an atheist?

On the way back to the dorm, I caught myself praying. It was a habit, a way of talking to myself without feeling insane. "God, please don't make me stop believing in you." Before the next class, I had a blinding insight. Infallibility, whereby the Pope cannot be wrong in matters of faith because he takes dictation directly from God: wasn't that as absurd as the emperor of Japan saying he was descended from the sun? The whole edifice crumbled for me—Father, Son, and Holy Ghost. (Was this what Dad was trying to prevent by keeping me in Ohio?) At any rate, I would discover that a person can describe herself as an atheist yet still maintain that, in the words of the Catechism, the Roman Catholic Church is the one true holy catholic and apostolic church.

The seal was off the milk bottle.

Soon I was registering for exotic-sounding courses like astronomy, existentialism, and mythology. I dropped astronomy (too much math) and was way over my head in existentialism, but mythology, Classics 355, was a revelation. It was a lecture class taught by Professor Froma Zeitlin, who assigned starry things like the *Oresteia* and the Homeric *Hymn to Demeter* and readings in Claude Lévi-Strauss, whose anthropological approach to myth was the basis of structuralism, and Mircea Eliade, a Romanian historian of religion, and Carl Jung, the Swiss psychiatrist who had developed a theory of archetypes (I thought it was pronounced "Archie types").

Professor Zeitlin was just starting her academic career and she already had a following. She was an inspired lecturer, who made mythology electrifying. In 1976, she moved to Princeton, where she taught for decades, gaining fame for the approach to classics that I had lucked into in the spring of my sophomore year. ("You studied with Froma Zeitlin?" a classicist asked me years later, awed.) She was particularly eloquent on the

"Great Round," the cycle of life and the seasons, and Gaia, the Earth Mother, as she deconstructed the myth of Demeter and Persephone and elaborated on the cult associated with them, the Eleusinian Mysteries.

Initiates into the cult walked in procession from Athens to Eleusis on a road known as the Sacred Way, along which were many tombs. Nobody knows precisely what the Mysteries were, but they had something to do with death. Eleusis was a center of worship of Demeter (De-*me*-ter), the patron goddess of agriculture. She was the Mother Nature of the Greek gods. Her daughter, Persephone—often called Kore, which means simply "girl"—was abducted by Hades and taken to the Underworld. Kore was out picking flowers and was attracted to an especially beautiful narcissus when Hades erupted from the earth in his horse-drawn chariot and carried her off. She was raped and abducted, and there was nothing anyone could do about it. Professor Zeitlin made it sound inevitable: "Virgins are always ripe for sacrifice." I was a virgin, and, like many coeds, I was eager to lose my virginity, but I had never thought of it that way.

The loss of her daughter was tragic for Demeter, who had no heart for making things grow anymore. No one could comfort her. She made the mortals suffer, too. If Mother Nature does not produce grain, if nothing germinates and nothing blooms, nobody eats. Demeter's grief caused a famine. Zeus and the other gods realized that if mortals were to go extinct, there would be no one to worship them—the gods are selfish—so he agreed to let the reluctant bride go back to her mother. But there was a trick: before she left, Hades made her eat a few seeds of a pomegranate. I don't think I knew what a pomegranate was before this, but it is a fruit of many seeds—it is a red globe crammed with red seeds, obscenely packed with seeds, a fruit that is nothing but seeds. Because she had eaten of the pomegranate—"she took his seed into her mouth"—Kore would have to return to the Underworld.

This was presented as the background for the Eleusinian Mysteries. People traveled on foot from Athens to Eleusis, past gravestones, thinking of a mother and daughter, of the inevitability of death and the promise of rebirth. Maddeningly, they were sworn to secrecy, and nobody revealed the content of the Mysteries. What happened when they got to Eleusis? Did they listen to a lecture, see a performance, close their eyes and follow a guided meditation? What did they learn? I wanted to be an initiate!

Professor Zeitlin was eloquent on the meaning of the myth as an explanation of the seasons: crops grow and are harvested and die back; trees lose their leaves and are bare all winter, but in the spring they send out sticky little leaves and revive our hopes. There was a time when people didn't know, couldn't trust, that spring would come. Frankly, every year, as winter lingers into April and May, *I* wonder if spring will come. So though it was a bleak scenario—rape, death, winter—it was a comfort to know there would be an end to suffering.

Professor Zeitlin's lecture culminated in the anthropological concept of the Great Round. The cycle of life begins with the earth and returns to the earth, the way the seasons revolve from life to death and back to life again. It doesn't mean that you don't suffer during the death part, or even the marriage part, but it does mean that as life gives way to death, death gives way to life again.

I went soaring out of Hickman Hall that spring day and ran down the lawn to catch the campus bus across town to Rutgers for Existentialism, slipped on the wet grass, flew up in the air, and landed on my ass in the mud. A woman who had been sitting at the top of the hill witnessed the scene and pointed at me, screaming with laughter. I cut Existentialism—probably missed Sartre's *Nausea*—and tromped back to the dorm, soggy but ecstatic.

I had spilled the milk. I was open to the Mysteries, excited about what came next, ready for a refill.

Professor Zeitlin's approach to mythology was different from anything I might have absorbed growing up. From *Ulysses* at the Lyceum in the 1950s to the blockbuster *Wonder Woman*, featuring an Amazon princess, in 2017, the appeal of mythology is timeless. The classic collections, if one may call them "classic" when they are directed at nonclassicists, include *Bulfinch's Mythology* and the encyclopedic two-volume *Greek Myths* compiled by Robert Graves, which offers so many variations on the exploits of gods and heroes that you may be tempted to make up your own. The latest addition is a collection called *Mythos* by the British author and actor Stephen Fry, who attributes his love of mythology to a book called *Tales from Ancient Greece*, which he picked up as a boy. In the popular Percy Jackson series by the American writer Rick Riordan, a twelve-year-old boy is immersed in fantasy adventures inspired by Greek mythology. Among all these approaches, the work that is perhaps the most accessible is that of Edith Hamilton, whose books *The Greek Way*, *The Roman Way*, and *Mythology* were extremely popular in mid-twentieth-century America and made her the interpreter of the Greeks for generations.

For many years, I thought of Hamilton as old-fashioned, as if that could possibly be a flaw in a writer on antiquity. I also had her confused with Margaret Hamilton, who played the Wicked Witch of the West in *The Wizard of Oz*. Both women lived on Gramercy Park for a while, and both are beloved and revered for their contributions to culture. Margaret Hamilton had that famous thin face and sharp chin and dark eyebrows (and, in the movie, a green complexion), and in the thumbnail portrait that appears on the back of my crumbling paperback copy of *The Greek Way*, Edith Hamilton bears a slight resemblance to her (lacking the iconic conical hat).

But Edith Hamilton was no witch (and, for that matter, neither was Margaret Hamilton). Edith Hamilton began to study Latin with her father when she was seven years old. Her paternal grandmother was an early proponent of education for women. Born in Germany in 1867, Edith grew up in Indiana, where she was homeschooled. She was sent to finishing school in Connecticut (Miss Porter's) before going abroad and, with her sister, becoming one of the first women to study at the University of Munich. She taught school for a living and did not begin to write about the Greeks until after she had retired as headmistress of the Bryn Mawr School, in Baltimore, when she was fifty-five.

Edith Hamilton had to be pushed into writing. She began with essays about the Greek tragedians for a theater magazine, and the writing was so lucid and engaging that she was encouraged to do more. Her collection *The Greek Way* was published in 1930 and was what is known in publishing circles as a sleeper: it sold steadily for years and years and is still in print today. From a lifetime of reading and teaching, Hamilton had digested the literature, in the original language, and could retell the stories in a spare and elegant style, without footnotes or any of the scholarly impedimenta that put off the general reader the same way that subtitles in foreign movies distract an American moviegoer. In *Mythology*, Hamilton's collection of Greek and Roman myths, she refers in a brief headnote to the authority she has chosen to follow, and then simply, even kindly, tells the story and offers some interpretation. Her language is clear and her message is illuminating.

One reason that Hamilton's work was so popular is that she made an end run around academia. Classicists cannot help being snobs: once you have read something in Greek, a translation is a pale imitation, almost a sacrilege. They would not themselves value the work of Edith Hamilton or Stephen Fry or Rick Riordan—or even of Robert Graves, though his encyclopedic scheme has the earmarks of scholarship. Yet these writers with the common touch are introducing mythology to people who may fall in love with it and go on to read Hesiod in Greek and Ovid in Latin. Something made me register for Classics 355, and whatever it was—those cheesy Hollywood movies at the Lyceum or Classics Illustrated from the rack at the drugstore— the allure of mythology was strong enough to lead me, in college, to that lecture class, which in turn, eventually, led me to Greek and Greece and to Eleusis.

TEN YEARS OUT OF COLLEGE, having at length lost my virginity, and undergone a revival of interest in mythology, I lit out along the Sacred Way for Eleusis, or Elefsina, as it's called in modern Greek. I wanted to see the tombs along the route and I hoped to experience something of what it felt like to be initiated into the Eleusinian Mysteries. Maybe by poking around on the sacred ground itself with my newly acquired modern Greek I could penetrate the mystery. At the least, I thought, I would see something of the countryside outside Athens.

I had timed my stay in Athens, against Dorothy Gregory's advice, to coincide with Greek Easter, which fell late that year, in May. I didn't understand that everything in the capital would be closed—the Greeks go to their ancestral villages or close up shop for days at a time. Wandering around in the Plaka, beneath the Acropolis, I saw a man turning a lamb on a spit in his patch of a backyard, and I longed to fit in somehow and celebrate the season. Perhaps in Elefsina, which in ancient times was sacred to Demeter, I would find something that would connect me to the pagan rites of spring.

From Athens to Elefsina is fourteen miles, and the Blue Guide, noting that "the first 3 or 4 miles are heavily industrialized and tedious to the pedestrian," recommended taking a bus. As a child of Cleveland and a former resident of the Garden State, I was not to be put off by "heavily industrialized." Fourteen miles sounded tedious, though. The Blue Guide mentioned that at Dafni (Δαφνή), six and three-quarters miles outside Athens, there was a monastery famous for its Byzantine mosaics. I decided to take the bus as far as Dafni and walk the Sacred Way from there.

My Greek language skills at the time were frail, but I was game. The words that most often left my lips were Δεν κατάλαβα (*Den katálava*)—"I don't understand." I would practice whatever question I needed to ask, but unless I got the answer I was hoping for, I didn't understand. Trying to get information about ferries from Crete to Rhodes, I was bold enough to telephone the equivalent of the port authority in Piraeus, but the man I talked to seemed to expect me to come back from Crete to Piraeus to go to Rhodes. It sounded as if every time I wanted to go somewhere I would have to start all over again. It was frustrating. Ferries existed only if the Greek you were talking to owned the ship or would receive a commission for selling you a ticket. (This was pre-Internet, remember, and the various ferry companies were not organized online for easy browsing.) After getting no satisfaction on the phone, despite having overcome my xenophonophobia (fear of foreign phones), I sought out the information kiosk at the port in Piraeus in person and posed my questions to the man there. I got the same unintelligible (or unacceptable) answer. "Δεν κατάλαβα," I said. The man's eyebrows shot up and he said, "I know you!" It was the same man I had spoken to on the phone.

On my Elefsinian expedition, all my Greek verbs somehow got jammed in the past tense, as if I were stuck in reverse. When I got on the bus, I asked the driver, "You took the Sacred Way to Elefsina?" Somewhat warily, he gave me the downward sideways nod of affirmation. What I saw from the bus window confirmed my suspicion that the Blue Guide exaggerated: suburbs of Athens, some large expanses of old tires, but nothing to compare to Cleveland or Elizabeth, New Jersey. We passed a basilica that I took for the monastery at Dafni—the Greeks on the bus crossed themselves repeatedly—and I got off. The bus driver gave me a quizzical look. "I walked," I explained. He grinned.

I walked, all right. I walked for more than an hour before I saw a sign for Dafni. The monastery was a leafy refuge behind a high stone wall. A handmade sign at the entrance said, "Closed Due to Damages from Earthquake." There had been a major earthquake in the Gulf of Corinth—6.7 on the Richter scale—in 1981, and apparently putting the mosaics back together again was not a priority.

Although I hadn't originally set out to visit the monastery and knew nothing about Byzantine mosaics, now that I was here I was not so easily turned away. Often it happens that a milestone, a stage on the journey, a name on the map chosen just to help me find my way somewhere else, becomes a destination in itself. So it was with Dafni. Now that I was here, I wanted in. Someone was on the other side of the wall, watering the garden. I made a racket at the gate with my meager vocabulary— "*Kaliméra*! Good morning! Is there nobody?"—and started the dogs barking. A man came to the gate, and I launched into a fractured monologue—"I was walking along the Sacred Way, and thought I'd ask for a little water . . ." I must have sounded like the Scarecrow chatting to the Wizard of Oz about running into Dorothy on the Yellow Brick Road. At least I knew how to say *neráki*, a little water, the diminutive of *neró*. The man was not impressed, and sent me over to a parking lot where some people were camping. The monastery, I learned, had been devoid of monks for years and was now a park and picnic site. The campers gave me a little water and asked if I was Finnish. I must have looked very pale.

"The new highway joins the ancient road in Dafni," the Blue Guide says. The modern highway, built in the sixties, is the toll road from Athens to Corinth, fifty miles west, and it was not intended for pedestrians. It reminded me of the FDR Drive, the busy highway along the East Side of Manhattan, which I accidentally rode my bicycle on once when I was new to New York, wobbling, terrified, along the narrow shoulder as traffic hurtled by, inches away from me. I would never make that mistake again. Now traffic whizzed past me on the Sacred Way, and every third vehicle—trucks, taxis, private cars—honked as it bore down on me from behind, shattering my nerves. Many drivers offered me a ride, but I declined. I watched for ancient tombs and instead saw miniature shrines in the shape of churches mounted on posts like rural mailboxes. Each held an icon, a wick in a shallow tin can, a pack of matches, and lamp oil, often in a recycled ouzo bottle. These were memorials to people who had been killed on the highway. It occurred to me, as another truck driver honked and shot past, that I might end up a casualty myself, and there would be nobody to raise a shrine for me.

I passed what looked like military installations, unphotogenic parcels of land with signs forbidding the taking of photographs (as if). Yellow-and-red triangles stamped with black exclamation points warned of danger ahead. A long, curving hill promised a view from the top: an oil refinery and rusty freighters in the Saronic Gulf, as it turned out. I passed factories that made equipment for telephone poles; stores selling huge assortments of colorful plastic merchandise, like sprinkling cans and laundry baskets; garden shops, where those mini churches were for sale; gas stations; more oil refineries. It was as if I were on the outskirts of some infernal industrial city like Gary, Indiana, except that here and there was a small olive grove. At one point, next to a stoneyard full of marble, there was a tiny working farm with chickens and Holsteins and bales of hay. Next to a convenience store for factory workers was a single ancient marble tomb with an olive tree spreading over it.

The surface of the Sacred Way was gummy with oil. My sandals had not been broken in when I started on the road, but they were now. My feet were coated with grease and dust. When I got to Elefsina, instead of going straight to the ruins I stopped in a *soupermarket*—Greeklish for a minimart—and bought a two-liter bottle of water and carried it with me to the ruins in a plastic bag. The sanctuary was not far from the center of town. Inside the gate, I started to sit down, but the Greek in the ticket booth wouldn't let me rest there. I was bad publicity. So I trudged up the hill behind the ruins and sat in the shade of some pine trees.

I took a long drink from my bottle of water and then stuck my bare feet in the plastic bag and poured the rest of the water over them. Ah . . . The crinkly plastic held—it did not leak. I suppose I should have had a higher purpose there as I looked out over the sanctuary of Ancient Eleusis and the flat roofs of modern Elefsina to the industrial cranes bending stiffly on the waterfront and the ships with rust to their watermarks and the storied island of Salamis, home of Ajax the Great, but just then I gave thanks for plastic. The word "plastic," after all, is from the Greek, and its original meaning was innocent enough: malleable, shape-shifting. A *zacharoplasteíon* (ΖΑΧΑΡΟΠΛΑΣΤΕΙΟΝ) is a pastry shop, or sugar shapery. The Greek for plastic wrap is διάφανη μεμβράνη—diaphanous membrane. Plastic is lightweight and versatile and practically indestructible (which, of course, is also its drawback). It keeps things from going bad. Plastic gets a bad rap. The very refineries I was looking at may have been the source of the plastic bag my feet were soaking in.

MOST OF WHAT WE KNOW about the Eleusinian Mysteries has been deduced from the Homeric *Hymn to Demeter*, which is among the earliest writings in Greek. The procession was held in the fall, at harvesttime. Initiates prepared for it in Athens (not the Athens in Ohio). One of the rites was that everyone drank a potion—a *kykeón* (the modern word means porridge or gruel)—of the sort that Demeter asked for when she came to Eleusis. Worn out by grief for her daughter and disguised as a mortal, she had stopped and sat down by a well. The daughters of the queen came along, and brought her home to their mother, Metanira, who took her on as a nanny to her newborn son. Metanira offered the goddess wine, but she declined and asked instead for barley water with mint, or pennyroyal (in the translation of Thelma Sargent, who was a *New Yorker* copy editor before my time). Edith Hamilton notes that Demeter requested the same cooling drink that farmers refreshed themselves with in the field. The authors of *The Road to Eleusis*, a book devoted to penetrating the Eleusinian Mysteries, believe that the active ingredient was "ergot of barley," a fungus that grows on wild grains. They write, "This potion—an hallucinogen—under the right set and setting, disturbs man's inner ear and trips astonishing ventriloquistic effects." The editor/translator of the volume of the Loeb Library devoted to the Homeric *Hymn to Demeter*, H. G. Evelyn-White, writes that the drinking of the potion, whatever it was, was an "act of communion" and "one of the most important pieces of ritual in the Eleusinian mysteries, as commemorating the sorrows of the goddess."

As Hamilton reminds us, in her spare and eloquent retelling of the myth, Demeter was one of the suffering gods. When her daughter went missing, she searched all over the earth. None of the gods would tell her what had happened, because it was with the consent of Zeus that Hades, his brother, had nabbed Persephone. Helios, the sun, had seen what happened, and when he told Demeter where her daughter was, and that it had all been arranged between the two brothers, she was so enraged that she left Olympus. No amount of persuasion could bring her back. The gods reminded her that Hades was actually a good catch. He is called Hades after the place where he reigns, the way someone in Shakespeare is called, say, Gloucester, but the god's real name is Pluto—Πλούτων, from πλούτος, meaning wealth—and he is rich in departed spirits. Think of him as an undertaker: even an undertaker needs a wife. And not all May-December marriages turn out badly.

Finally, with mankind on the brink of extinction, Zeus agreed to give Demeter's daughter back. That's where the pomegranate came into play: having eaten the food of the Underworld, the girl would have to go back there every year. Like her mother, she, too, suffers, because although she returns with the flowers of spring, she is never innocent again.

Kore has the sweetness of a girl. She does not have much personality—her epithet in the Homeric *Hymn to Demeter* is slim-ankled—but she was popular: the hymn provides a catalogue of the friends who were out there picking flowers with her the day Hades swooped in. Her freshness is inspiring, enviable. I thought of Kore/Persephone when I read *Anne of Green Gables* while visiting Prince Edward Island, where most of the Anne books by Lucy Maud Montgomery are set. Sometimes when I am on a grassy trail through a meadow bordered by roses, with Queen Anne's lace and goldenrod waving in the breeze, I can still feel some of the freshness of a young girl's response to spring. But a girl has to grow up, right?

Perhaps the initiates, too, freshened up before entering the sanctuary of Demeter at Eleusis. I climbed down from the piney hill and started up the home stretch of the Sacred Way. In ancient times, I would have been in a crowd of excited Greeks of all classes. The only other people here now, however, were a party of French tourists. I envied them because they had someone telling them about the rocks, interpreting for them. I was an archaeological illiterate. But here is what I saw, armed with the Blue Guide: The well by which Demeter sat down when she came to Eleusis was still here. Broad, shallow marble steps rose to a propylaeum, or forecourt, and turned in toward the hill. Poppies and broom and sea lavender bloomed among the ruins. On my right was the Cave of Hades, a natural grotto in the hillside. This may have been where Persephone, as she might be called once she is Queen of the Underworld, emerged, blinking, in the spring. It's not explicit in the myth, but she must have been pregnant, because she was raped by a god, and gods can't not be potent. (The place of her rape has been associated with a field in Sicily.) Here were temples to Aphrodite and Poseidon. Past several lobbies where perhaps souvenirs were sold, or people gathered as in any lobby before an event, at the very end of the Sacred Way, was the holiest place: the Hall of the Initiates, a square space, roofless now, the floor paved with slabs of stone, before bleacher-like stands cut into the rocky hillside.

This is where it happened, whatever it was. Arriving at the

inner sanctum, the initiates would not have seen as many gas stations or as much rust as I did. They would have passed a field of grain at harvesttime. Pausanias, touring Eleusis in the first century AD, wrote, "Here they show you Triptolemos's threshing-floor and altar." Triptolemos, a prince of Eleusis, was the first, Pausanias says, to "sow cultivated grain." This was written almost two thousand years ago, but as little as two hundred years ago, in 1801, the site was still a center of worship of Demeter. That year, an enterprising and unscrupulous traveler from England, one E. D. Clarke, made off with a two-ton *kistophoros*—a feminine statue resembling a caryatid holding a basket on her head—against the protests of the villagers. Peter Levi, in his notes to Pausanias, writes that "an ox ran up, butted the statue repeatedly, and fled bellowing." Clarke's treasure sank in a shipwreck off Beachy Head, in East Sussex, England. The statue from the sanctuary of Demeter was eventually salvaged and installed in Cambridge.

In the years since my pilgrimage to Elefsina, I have learned that back in the sixties and seventies, when Greece was governed by a right-wing junta whose members were known as the Colonels, there was a flowering of petroleum refineries and other polluting industries in the Gulf of Salamis, at the foot of the city sacred to agriculture. Elefsina has long had a reputation among Greeks as the city that was ruined by industrial development. It is as if the whole region had been raped, despoiled, sacrificed. Talk about having to accept death in the midst of life. A plastic bag is handy, but can it really have been worth it to trade off the sanctuary of the goddess of agriculture for plastic? I had the feeling, standing in the Hall of the Initiates, under the hillside that protected the site, that Demeter had left the building.

"The dream forbids me to write what lies inside the sanctuary wall," Pausanias goes on to say, "and what the uninitiated are not allowed to see they obviously ought not to know about." Earlier, in Athens, Pausanias had visited the Eleusinion, an Athenian sanctuary presumably sacred to Demeter, and he writes that he wanted to "describe the contents . . . but I was stopped by something I saw in a dream. I must turn to the things it is not irreligious to write for general readers." The trail of the content of the Mysteries goes cold there, back in the early Roman era.

One of the loveliest things I saw at Elefsina was a stele, or grave marker, showing a relief of a seated woman with a little girl at her knee. The woman was straight-backed; the child, trusting, holds something out to her. It was the only image I saw at Elefsina that might be interpreted as an illustration of the mother love that is so abundant in the myth. Back home, I had been struck, over the past several years, observing some of my friends as young mothers, by the affection between mother and daughter. I don't remember ever experiencing that as a girl, except with my grandmother, when she held me on her lap and read to me—probably the beginning of my love of reading. My early childhood coincided with dark days in our house. My mother, like Demeter, had lost a child. He was a boy, named Patrick, and he was two years older than me. I have no memory of Patrick himself, but I grew up hearing my mother tell the story of the day he died, in all its detail, over and over, implanting the family mythology. It was March—a bad month—and Patrick was just a few weeks shy of his third birthday. There was bacon for breakfast. My mother told Patrick to wait, that she would cut up his bacon for him as soon as she was finished feeding the baby. But he didn't wait, and he choked on a piece of bacon. My father was there at the breakfast table, and he turned Patrick upside down and whacked him on the back, trying to dislodge it. (Nobody yet knew about the Heimlich maneuver, now posted by law in every restaurant.) It was all my father knew to do, but it didn't work.

My mother would go on to describe my father's grief, how he never talked about it during the day, but at night, in bed, he would sob, his whole body shaking. He even went to see the parish priest and ask for help, and the priest said that they should have another baby. So they had my little brother. "But my heart wasn't in it," my mother would say. She would say it right in front of the child who was conceived to replace Patrick. (And I thought I had it bad.) Who could compete with the broad-shouldered auburn-haired boy in the maroon corduroy shirt with the troubled little face who lived in the tinted photograph on our parents' dresser? His funeral things—a lock of hair and a wreath—were kept in a long flat box at the back of the kitchen closet. They couldn't find his shoes, my mother said, the shoes had disappeared, so he was buried without them. When we got back on Friday nights from driving my grandmother home after her weekly visit, we would stand out on the back porch and look up at the stars and ask my mother, "Which one is Patrick's star?" She would point one out.

It was not until years later that I realized I felt guilty for my brother's death—if it hadn't been for my presence there at the breakfast table, he wouldn't have died. I spent my childhood in the impossible position of having to try to console my inconsolable mother. We were both too worn out for me to learn or for her to teach me anything practical or domestic. I couldn't scramble an egg or get a stain out of a shirt. By the time I got to college and took that course in mythology, I was still helpless, stubbornly protesting my innocence.

Somehow that mythology course with Professor Zeitlin was the beginning of releasing me from guilt. Professor Zeitlin, in her lecture on the Eleusinian Mysteries, had pointed out that the ravishing of Kore combines in one act the three rites of passage of womanhood: birth, marriage, and death. In being raped, Kore dies as a maiden daughter and is born as Persephone, Queen of the Underworld. At the time, I identified with Kore— I was a virgin, I gloried in the lilacs blooming around the edges of the cul de sac of cozy gray houses that served as our dormitory. I was a flower child. That campus was the meadow that Kore was playing in with her friends when Hades erupted out of the earth and came for her. Until that day in the lecture hall, I had been afraid to grow up, to trade in my girlhood for the life of a woman.

Professor Zeitlin's class had woken me to the fact that I could have other models: be a bitch, be a huntress, be an Amazon, be a maenad, one of the crazed followers of Dionysus. Mythology taught me that I didn't have to limit myself to virgin, bride, and mother—there were many other roles to play. I didn't have to be like my mother and wear a girdle every day of my life, I didn't have to be constrained. I could let myself live.

Now, here at Elefsina, where I'd hoped to have some kind of spring fling, I realized that I had my mother in me after all, and I was glad of it. Women are the continuum. My mother, in her unbearable sadness, went on to make breakfast for us every day, to bear another child, and though my younger brother and I have never had children ourselves, our older brother married a corn goddess (my sister-in-law is from Iowa) and they have two fine boys, both musicians, one named Patrick. Miles is a gardener, something he never learned from our father, who seemed to go out of his way to trample my mother's chrysanthemums when he painted the house. I came to Greece to get away from my family, but as I set my course for Athens again, they were with me. This time, I took the bus.

# CHAPTER 5

# A TASTE FOR TRAGEDY

B Y MY MID-THIRTIES, I was deep into classical Greek. At *The New Yorker*, I had settled into my job on the copydesk and was training a series of copy editors, trying to move up to the next level, but reluctant to give up a night shift that allowed me to have days free for my extracurricular activities. The magazine was moving toward a takeover by the Newhouses, who owned *Vogue*, *Vanity Fair*, and a lot of other magazines, and speculation about who would succeed William Shawn as the editor-in-chief was ramping up. *The New Yorker* had been stable for decades—Shawn had been editor since the year I was born, 1952—and we were afraid that new owners would fiddle with our traditions. No. 1 pencils? Tuition reimbursement? Some of the older employees, like Ed Stringham, had settled into well-worn grooves, and it was hard to picture a new owner putting up with them. Shawn's shop was home to many eccentrics, one of whom I was on the path to becoming.

I had registered for Elementary Greek at Barnard, choosing a section taught by a venerable classics professor named Helen Bacon. This was a historic opportunity: she was teaching beginners for the last time. But when Professor Bacon defined Hesperus, the evening star (Venus), with reference to the Latin Vespers, prayers at dusk, I could not take her point. It offended me that Greek should be taught through Latin when I was illiterate in that dead language but brimming with modern Greek. I crossed the street to Columbia and enrolled in a section taught by a professor new to Columbia, Laura Slatkin.

Professor Slatkin was a native New Yorker, educated at Brearley, Radcliffe, and Cambridge, who had come to Columbia on a Mellon Fellowship. She was an Athena type, witty, serious, and attractive, with great winged eyebrows. She would joke that students who came to class unprepared were responsible for the premature gray in her hair. I was closer in age to her than I was to the undergraduates, but that didn't mean we could pal around. She gave the class an occasional glimpse into her private life. One day she told us that a friend had given birth the night before—she had attended—and the word "contractions," which we had encountered in certain verbs in ancient Greek, had taken on new and urgent meaning. She laughingly described the efforts of three PhDs to follow the manufacturer's instructions to assemble a crib.

Unlike the undergraduates, who were enrolled in organic chemistry and advanced Latin and statistics and the Great Books course that Columbia is famous for—along with rowing crew and making art and smoking dope and screwing around— I had only one class to prepare for, and no social life, with the result that I was able to devote myself completely to my studies, coming out of my Greek swoon for a few hours a day to go to the office and copy-edit for the purpose of paying the rent.

Traditionally, the first text that Greek students grapple with is Xenophon's *Anabasis*, which records the long march upcountry (anabasis means "going up") and the retreat of ten thousand (a myriad) Greek mercenary soldiers who fought in Persia from 401 to 399 BC. It is mostly about how many parasangs they cover every day—a parasang, according to Herodotus and Xenophon, is equal to 30 stadiums, or about five and a half kilometers—slogging along in the desert, up hills, over rocks, over more rocks, up more hills, until finally they see the sea and shout, "*Thálassa! Thálassa!*" ("The sea! The sea!") At last they are as good as home. Professor Slatkin skipped the *Anabasis* and instead gave us Plato's *Apology of Socrates*, which is about the trial and death of Socrates at the hands of the state. She knew how to make a person fall in love with ancient Greek. She also used a new textbook, Hansen and Quinn, which she said was an improvement on the textbook she had learned Greek from, in which the sample sentences were all about moving rocks from one side of the road to the other. The first day's homework was to copy a list of Greek words printed in lowercase—ἥλιος, Ὅμηρος (sun, Homer)—in all capitals (ΗΛΙΟΣ, ΟΜΗΡΟΣ). It was surprisingly useful, and learning the words was an enticement to read outside the textbook.

After a year of Elementary Greek with Professor Slatkin, I registered for her course in Greek Tragedy. We met on the sixth floor of Hamilton Hall. I swear you needed an advanced degree just to find your classroom, because Columbia counted the basement (and the subbasement, if there was one) as a floor. The Hamilton for whom the building was named was Alexander, of course, a famous alumnus who had dropped out during the Revolutionary War, and it looked as if it might have been built in his day. The roof leaked, and chunks of the ceiling rained down. Professor Slatkin was pleased to be able to say, with some flair, "*Après moi, le déluge.*"

At the time, I was living in Astoria, above two Italian-American brothers in the semidetached brick house they had grown up in, and I would sit at a table by my second-floor window early in the morning, like a monk at his devotions, looking up occasionally as a train rolled over the viaduct leading to the Hell Gate Bridge, with my Greek text and my spiral notebooks and my abridged Liddell and Scott, a gift from my little brother.

Professor Slatkin had suggested that, with my limited Greek, I elect something easier—Herodotus was on offer across the street, at Barnard—but I had developed a taste for tragedy. Maybe it was self-dramatization, maybe it was melodrama, but I had an intimation that whatever we read in Greek Tragedy would put my own troubles in perspective. Professor Slatkin had chosen the two plays that she believed no one should graduate from college without having read: *Antigone* and *Oedipus Tyrannus* (which classicists refer to as the *OT*), both by Sophocles. *Antigone* took up most of the semester, and we squeezed *Oedipus* into a few weeks at the end, with Professor Slatkin handing out sheets of vocabulary notes to save us time delving in the lexicon.

I was the class nerd. I copied the Greek text painstakingly into my notebook, about ten lines at a time, observing every diacritical mark, and covered the facing page with vocabulary notes—verbs with their principal parts, nouns with their genders and genitives—and, after negotiating the twists and turns of syntax, penciled in a frail translation of Sophocles. It was thrilling to see the meaning emerge, to observe the subtle uses of tense and aspect and mood, and to feel the force of the untranslatable particles.

There are words in *Antigone* that are current in English today—*miasma* is one—and words that are the roots from which English words have sprung. For instance, *hérpo* means "to creep, glide," and has given us herps, as in herpetology, the study of reptiles—snakes, salamanders, and other creeping things. The verb *speíro* means to sow or scatter, and, combined with the prefix *dia* (across, through), yields diaspora, a scattering across or throughout. History has given us the Jewish diaspora, the Greek diaspora, and the Diaspora Club, as a group of soon-to-be-former *New Yorker* editors would call themselves.

I also lapped up the specialized vocabulary of classicists. They had a name for everything! "Oh, that's a hapax legomenon," someone might say, meaning a word that occurred a single time in a given author. *Hysteron proteron* ("later before") meant saying what should follow first. My favorite was lacuna, a gap in the text where a worm had eaten a hole in the papyrus. And we were all prone to the occasional haplography, a scribal error in which the copyist's eye fell on the second use of a word, causing him to omit the lines between the first and second uses. Scholars also had a convention that encouraged them, when it was unclear which of two manuscript readings was authentic, to favor the more difficult or unusual option. I found this perverse, in a good way. There were also notes on poetic form and meter, and exercises in scansion. All this to love before even touching on plot or character!

The text we were using for *Antigone* was the work of Richard Claverhouse Jebb, of Cambridge University. For 47 pages of Greek, it had 186 pages of English commentary—abridged from a much larger work, published in 1900. Classicists call it, simply, Jebb. I carried Jebb around with me like a favorite doll, puzzling over it on the train when I went to visit friends in Boston and holding it open on my lap when we were playing bridge, hoping that while I wasn't looking, some of the words would rearrange themselves into meaningful units, like letters in an anagram, and jump out at me.

Most people know the story of Antigone. The daughter of Oedipus buries her brother Polynices—or at least throws a handful of dust on his body to ensure safe passage to the Underworld—disobeying her uncle Creon, the new king of Thebes, and earning the death penalty. Antigone is a spitfire, defying Creon in the serene belief that she is obeying a higher law. If Antigone did not soar like a phoenix above this tragedy, it would be Creon's play. He needs to be right, and by the time Tiresias enters (always bad news) and the chorus of Theban elders persuades Creon to admit he's wrong, it is too late. His niece Antigone has hanged herself; his son Haemon, who was betrothed to Antigone (yes, they were cousins), kills himself, whereupon his wife, Eurydice, Haemon's mother, also kills herself, leaving Creon broken and alone.

One of the things that impressed me about Sophocles was the way this play is over even before it begins: at the protagonist's entrance we are already looking at the consequences of what she is about to do, and everything from there on is drawn in unsparing detail, so that we know just how it feels to be Antigone. In one speech, which I was able to translate almost magically, as if I had written it myself (it is thought by some to be spurious), she enlarges on the value of a brother, making the point that if a husband or a child dies, one can remarry or have another child, but a brother engendered by parents who are no longer alive can never be replaced. I thought I understood, and I am not talking about my brother Patrick. I had two other brothers, one older and one younger, and I was particularly close to my younger brother. I felt as if I were losing him, though not to death. That year, my year of Antigone, my brother did the unthinkable: he got married. It brought to an end the years of our youth: both of us in New York, hanging out together, with a shared set of references and inside jokes. I admit that he filled in for the social life I didn't have. He was funny and wise, and I preferred his company to anyone else's. Once, we were introduced to a friend's cousin, an interesting guy, who called the next day to make a date with *me*—I actually held the phone away from my ear and looked at it as if to say, "Are you sure? My brother is much better company." I forgot that, to a heterosexual man, I, as a woman, might be more attractive than my brother.

Sometimes you read something at exactly the right time, whether it's a classic you missed in childhood that would have been wasted on you as an eight-year-old (I read *The Wind in the Willows* and *Charlotte's Web* in bed with my lover in college) or something that you were too snooty to read when it first came out—Richard Ford's *The Sportswriter*—that speaks to you profoundly once you give up your pose of superiority. (Ford made me change my mind about discretionary commas.) A great book about the Donner Party (*Desperate Passage*) can make you resolve to never waste a scrap of food again. Who you are when you come to a book (*Raise High the Roof Beam,*

*Carpenters*) can give you an intimate experience that you would not have had if that book was assigned in class, if you *had* to read it. I might have felt sorry for myself for not getting Latin early and for being in my thirties by the time I found Greek, but I knew that what I brought to it—in the case of *Antigone*, my history with my brother—was making it hit me in a way that it wouldn't have when I was younger. What happened was not even happening to me—I just experienced the fallout of things that were happening to others—but the extreme experience of Antigone (remember, her brother was also her nephew) helped me cope with the feeling of being sidelined in my own family.

And here we have a riddle worthy of the Sphinx: What goes by the masculine pronoun in youth, the feminine pronoun in middle age, and the singular "they" in old age? My hermaphrodite. After playing Antigone at my brother's wedding, I took on the role again when my brother, like Tiresias, changed gender, and began a new life as a female. I resisted the word "sister." I had not had a sister when I needed one, and I didn't want one now, especially when it was someone who was trying to take my brother's place. It is not unusual, I learned, for a person to experience a family member's change of gender as a death, which is very disturbing to the transitioner, who feels she is being reborn. "It's not nice to hear you're dead," my brother said. For me, at first, his transformation seemed like a rejection of our shared past. I would learn to use the feminine pronoun in the present, but when I was talking about the past

I felt entitled to revert to the masculine. But this was several years in the future. For now, I had lost access through marriage to my boon companion and it felt as good as death—or as bad. Things would never be the same.

In class, Professor Slatkin gave a different scholarly article to each student of Greek tragedy and asked us to write a response. Mine was about Antigone's motive: Why did she do it? I was aghast to discover that there was an entire body of literature devoted to this question. To me it was perfectly obvious why Antigone did it: she loved her brother. She did what came naturally to her, and to be faulted for that can elicit no repentance because there was nothing to repent: she couldn't have done it differently. She was blameless. The only other thing I had read in classical Greek at that point was Plato's *Apology*, and I saw parallels between Antigone and Socrates: both were martyred by the state for being married to the truth.

THE PURSUIT OF GREEK TRAGEDY can actually have a happy ending. Or at least it can end in relief. It was around that time, while taking Elementary Greek, that I saw a notice on campus announcing auditions for a production of Euripides' *Electra* in ancient Greek. Having never studied a dead language before, I missed the social aspects of language learning—eating ethnic food, writing skits, improvising dialogues—and this might be as close as I could get to conversational ancient Greek. So I tried out. A fair-haired graduate student listened to me read a passage from the Homeric *Hymn to Demeter* and said, "I'd love to have you in the chorus."

Performance of Greek drama in the original language (or some semblance of it) is a long-standing academic tradition. In 1881, students at Harvard University staged *Oedipus Tyrannus* in the original Greek, a production that was seen by six thousand people. The Barnard Columbia Greek Drama Group—now the Barnard Columbia Ancient Drama Group—was founded in the 1976–77 academic year, with a production of Euripides' *Medea*. A student named Matthew Alan Kramer, who was in the play, was killed in an accident that summer, and his family set up a memorial fund "for the promotion of these plays, which he loved." I had seen their production of *The Cyclops*, a satyr play by Euripides, before my first trip to Greece. It opened with the title character lumbering onstage and sitting down at a harpsichord to play a winsome piece by Rameau titled "Les Cyclopes." I was enchanted.

For the first read-through of *Electra*, in English, we met at the director's apartment, on one of the long blocks of apartment buildings and fraternity houses just south of Columbia. Each of us brought a different translation. I got the impression that this was not one of Euripides' greatest hits. Electra and Orestes sounded like brats hatching a juvenile plot to kill Mom. Our Electra, a graduate student named Lavinia, had a regal bearing and an impressive academic pedigree: her mother was a Dante scholar, and her father a mathematician. The student playing Orestes, who bore a slight resemblance to Gregory Peck, had played the part before, in the *Eumenides*, with Lavinia as Athena. The undergraduate who competed with Lavinia for the role of Electra had been cast as Clytemnestra and would get killed by her.

The chorus was made up of milk-fed Mycenaean girls who drop by to invite Electra to a procession at the temple of Hera. There were four of us: a classics major named Hilary, who, though somewhat stiff onstage, had read a lot of Greek and was asked to lead the chorus; a cherubic blonde who had devised her own major in Byzantine studies; a Greek-American who, despite her heritage, was unfamiliar with the House of Atreus and was horrified to learn what Electra and Orestes were up to; and me.

The director distributed sheet music and audiocassettes of the odes to help us learn the Greek. The chorus would rehearse separately from the rest of the cast, with a choreographer. No decision had been made about the musical accompaniment, but I gave the producer the number of my brother (as he was at the time), who played the harp.

The first hurdle for the chorus was memorizing the lines. We were using a scheme of restored pronunciation, which I was scornful of. I held the ignorant opinion that it would make more sense to follow the pronunciation of contemporary Greeks than that of scholars and linguists from Cambridge or Yale, though

I liked the restored pronunciation of *oi*, as in "*Oi moi*," a typical exclamation in tragedy, meaning something like "Woe is me" or the Yiddish "*Oy vey*." Many vowels and vowel combinations from ancient Greek have been streamlined in the modern language and are all pronounced the same. Or, as James Merrill puts it, rather negatively, in his early novel *The (Diblos) Notebook*, "The modern Greek language can be said to have suffered a stroke. Vowels, the full *oi*'s & *ei*'s of classical days, have been eclipsed to a waning, whining *ee*."

You don't so much read ancient Greek as construe it, teasing out the different strands and seeing which parts of a sentence go together. English sentences tend to follow a predictable subject-verb-object pattern. In a Greek sentence, an adjective at the end can modify a noun at the beginning, and the words can pile up in between like a pyramid with the crucial verb at the top. We had five convoluted choral odes and a lament to master, and I spent hours thumbing through the Greek lexicon and comparing translations. The official translation for the production was Emily Townsend Vermeule's, but I noticed that the director carried around a prose translation by Moses Hadas, who had taught at Columbia. It seemed that classicists preferred literal translations. A translator who tried to replicate the Greek meter produced unidiomatic—not to say tortured—English. Greek just does things differently from English. Enough exposure to Greek will do two things: it will make a snob out of you, because you see that no translation approaches the beauty and subtlety of the original, and it will provoke you to prove yourself wrong by attempting your own translation, which will not be universally admired.

The choreography for the odes had to be simple, because we were not dancers, and it had to communicate the meaning as literally as possible, because not everyone in the audience would be a Greekist. We were like backup singers, waving our arms around, acting out sphinxes and rowing invisible boats and bringing the axe down on Agamemnon's neck in a retelling of his murder in the bath. The director implored us to get the lines down cold, so that if there was any kind of distraction during the performance—if the set collapsed or an ambulance wailed up Amsterdam Avenue—we could sail over it unperturbed.

One night my brother showed up at rehearsal with his harp. The producer had called him, and he had met with the director. "He is exactly the kind of guy who is not cut out for this job," my brother said, laughing. The director was visibly nervous: it emerged that his academic survival depended on his passing exams that spring, and instead of studying he was putting on a show. At the first musical rehearsal, he conducted with a Bic pen, making abrupt, exaggerated gestures, and watched helplessly as someone grabbed a page from his score, which had been taped together into one long document, and unspooled it across the floor. Outside of rehearsal, I helped my brother with the Greek, transliterating the words and defining them, so that even if he couldn't construe a line, he knew what the words sounded like and which ones were important. He did every pragmatic thing he could to make sure that nothing he had control over would go wrong during the performance. He had his score reduced and glued it to cardboard so that it wouldn't slip off the music stand. He made a tuning chart for the harp. He bought new black clothes, like a costume, to shore up his confidence.

We started rehearsing with the principals to learn our cues. Electra had an opening aria, which Lavinia sang in a reedy, affecting voice, and she and Orestes had a duet at the end, with the chorus joining in for the ritual lament, or kommos. "I want this to be really *terrible*," the director said, meaning shocking and bloodthirsty, like a chainsaw massacre. After all, Clytemnestra was an axe murderer.

My brother and I usually left rehearsal together, stopping at a bar on the way home, where he would badger me to keep rehearsing when I just wanted to drink. One day he went off to practice with Lavinia instead, and I headed down Broadway alone. I was inwardly repeating the ode for a scene in which the chorus celebrates the return of Orestes, when Orestes himself rounded the corner with the director. I opened my mouth and Greek fell out: "Ἔμολες ἔμολες, ὤ . . ." They understood me perfectly—"You've come, you've come, O long-awaited day. You shine, you show forth, you appear in the city a torch!"—and invited me to join them for pizza.

Euripides was turning my life inside out: I was living in the text, going over my lines every spare moment, in the tub and on the subway and in bed at night. I neglected to pay my bills or water my plants or do the dishes. I reported, as usual, to my job on the copydesk, but I sometimes had the sensation that I was an alien from Argos plunked down in the hallway of a seedy midtown office. Our system of rolling up proofs and inserting them into a Plexiglas-and-leather canister and shooting it up a pneumatic tube to the production department, two floors above, for transmission by fax to the printer, in Chicago, seemed suddenly quaint, even to me. How much longer could this go on?

One night I dreamed that I was handling shards, pieces of ancient pottery with writing on them. The dream came back to me as I passed a church on the way to rehearsal, and I realized that ancient Greek is like the Bible (from βίβλος): records of the past that preserve the things that humans most need to know.

FINALLY IT WAS opening night at the Teatro Piccolo, in Columbia's Casa Italiana, a building furnished with massive fake antiques that were rumored to have been sent over by Mussolini in lieu of a cash donation. Over the stage was a quote from Virgil. The floor was strewn with hay, as for a children's Nativity pageant. The chorus, wearing peploi—ankle-length tubes of crinkly fabric, in red, yellow, blue, and orange, pinned at the shoulders—sat in the back row, waiting for our entrance. When the harpist cued us with four repeated bars, we squeezed one another's hands, willing our synapses to connect and feed us the lines, and surged up the aisle.

Because I was the only one who remembered the words, I had an impromptu solo during the reenactment of Agamemnon's death cry: "Will you murder me?" Clytemnestra screamed, there was a tumult backstage, and Electra and Orestes entered red-handed. The bodies were hauled onstage, and the effect was as chilling and incongruous in the childlike Nativity-play setting as the director could have wished. The play ended with Castor and Polydeuces, twin brothers of Clytemnestra and Helen, appearing, not from above (there was no money in the budget for a crane) but from the wings, to denounce the matricide. Castor was played by a Greek Cypriot, Demetrios Ioannides, who rolled out his lines with the godlike authority of someone speaking his mother tongue.

The audience was disappointingly small for an event that had reached epic proportions in my brain. "Euripides' *Electra*," the flyers proclaimed: "Fun for the Whole Family!" We performed four times, Thursday to Saturday, with a matinee on Friday; no performance was perfect. My brother and I alternated in being elated or dejected after each show. I complained that I felt no magic. "That's too bad, but nobody cares how you feel," my brother said. "It doesn't have to be magic for you but could still be magic for the audience."

On the last night, Ed Stringham brought some people from the office—I was his protégée, after all—so there was a *New Yorker* contingent in the audience. Who knew how much longer the magazine would support an employee's avocation as a Greek chorus girl? I had persuaded the people in Goings On About Town to run a little blurb for us. Both my Greek teachers, Dorothy Gregory and Laura Slatkin, were there, along with a contingent of classics scholars, who, the director had said, would be able to construe the odes as we were singing them. I was nervous. That night, we the chorus stumbled at our entrance, two of us counting wrong and the other two stubbornly setting it right. But it was OK. As when a brand-new Plymouth Fury incurs a fender bender on its first outing, the pressure of perfection was off. We were freer after that, more forgiving. Between the odes, I concentrated on listening to the dialogue. Even if I couldn't understand what Electra and Orestes and Clytemnestra were saying, I could listen to the sound of the Greek. At every performance, I understood more—isolated words, genitive endings, a vocative inflection (Clytemnestra's "ὦ παῖ"—"O child"). Toward the end, just before Clytemnestra walked into the trap set by her darlings, Orestes and Electra came downstage and argued, and I distinctly heard Orestes whine to his sister, "But I don't want to kill Mom." I also heard Electra's answer, and what she said didn't make sense, but it didn't make sense *in Greek*. It was not supposed to make sense. She was telling him why he had to kill his mother, compelling him to go through with it, defying a law that was older and holier than her need for retribution: Thou shalt not kill—especially thy mother.

Still, I had some sympathy for Electra. The way I saw it, she had no choice. She hated her mother and could not rest until Clytemnestra was dead. But once she had killed her, everything would be worse instead of better. It was as if you had something in your eye that drove you crazy, and instead of trying to distract yourself from it or somehow live with it, you gouged it out, only to realize that having something in your eye was nowhere near as bad as not having the eye at all.

I told Professor Slatkin about my epiphany after our next class, and she said it was a good example of anagnorisis: a term from Aristotle that means a turning point in the action of a play when a character recognizes some truth about himself. Orestes rejects Electra's scheme—he knows it's wrong—but she bullies him into it anyway. In a very small way, I saw our family in this scene: my attempts as a child to bend my brother to my will, to enlist his sympathy against our mother. Fortunately, he resisted. And no blood was shed in the House of Norris.

My career as a tragedienne peaked the following year, when I was plucked from the chorus of *Electra* and given the lead in *The Trojan Women*. It was Euripides again, and the part was Hecuba, the Queen of Troy. I had been hoping to play Cassandra—a walk-on as a madwoman would have suited me perfectly—but, as a thirty-three-year-old "postgraduate special student," I was cast in the role of the hag while the part of the ingénue went to a slinky undergraduate. The shrewd student-director told me that if I didn't play Hecuba the role would go to Hilary, of last year's chorus. I couldn't let *that* happen.

Hecuba carries the play. It opens with her lying on the ground after the defeat of Troy. She has lost her son Hector and her husband, King Priam. This is the end, the tragic aftermath of the Trojan War as seen by the women of Troy. Again, the plot is linear: Cassandra and Andromache, Hector's wife, sweep in and out; Helen, Hecuba's archenemy, makes an appearance, reunited with her husband, Menelaus; the body of young Astyanax, Hector's heir, who was flung from the towers of Troy by the Greeks lest he survive to reclaim the kingdom, is handed over to his grandmother. Talthybius, Agamemnon's herald, played by my Greek Cypriot friend Demetrios, grows in sympathy for Hecuba. The play is an exercise in comparative and superlative: Hecuba starts out sad and gets sadder and sadder and *sadder* until she is the saddest woman who ever lived.

The role was a feat of memorization. Each scene came with a long speech—forty or more lines of Greek. I started with the last speech, the one over the body of Astyanax, because I knew that if I learned the speeches in order the last one would suffer, and it was both the climax and the low point of Hecuba's misfortunes. I had been able to identify with Electra, because I was a daughter and a sister, but what was Hecuba to me? She was a wife and mother, and a queen. One of my father's nicknames for my mother was Queen.

I did not have to look far for a model of grief over a lost child. I could still hear my mother's stories: how, after Patrick's funeral, bewildered, I had toddled over to my father's knee, perhaps to say, "I'm still here—what about me?" and he had said, "You're a good kid, Mary." And I had my own searing memory of my baby brother greeting me at the door one day, worried, to say, "Mom got out Patrick's funeral things and cried." He and I had been trying all our lives to account for the ways we were shaped by our brother's death.

I devoted a day to construing the speech over Astyanax and storing it in my memory, adding a line at a time, until by evening I had a huge undigested wad of Greek in my system. I felt like a snake that had swallowed a piglet. I photocopied all the speeches and glued them to index cards, so that Hecuba was always in my pocket. When I swam laps at the pool, I added a line per lap. The last chunk I memorized was the furious speech to Helen, which scared the cat off my lap: she couldn't understand why I was so angry. Euripides used to be relegated to third place, behind Aeschylus and Sophocles, in the hierarchy of the Greek tragic playwrights, but he knew what he was doing. As long as I didn't panic, all I had to do if I forgot a line was think of what would logically come next, and there it was.

I worried about how to pace the sadness so that there would still be somewhere to go by the time I got to Astyanax. Katharine Hepburn had played Hecuba in a 1971 movie version of *The Trojan Women*. I was a fan of Hepburn, making a point of going to revivals of her films at the Thalia, but I had missed *The Trojan Women*, and I didn't dare watch it now, when I had to play the role myself, in a dead language, without her cheekbones. I decided to write her a letter. I knew she lived in Turtle Bay, in the East Forties, where E. B. White once lived, but a young editor who had recently come to *The New Yorker* from Knopf, which was publishing Hepburn's memoir about the making of *The African Queen*, told me that Hepburn would be alarmed to think that a stranger knew where she lived, and that it would be better to approach her obliquely, through her publisher. "Dear Katharine Hepburn," I wrote, and told her my problem—that I had to play Hecuba in Greek—and made a lofty reference to Bartók and a Hungarian folk song that was piercingly sad and beautiful, something about a tree. I asked Ms. Hepburn how she had varied her performance. I had had a little experience in musical comedy, but was it possible, in tragedy, to play it for laughs?

Not long afterward, I got an answer. It was a typewritten note on letterhead stationery, dated January 15, 1985, with the name Katharine Houghton Hepburn engraved in red. "Dear Mary Jane Norris," it began. (I had insisted on using my Catholic-school name on this occasion to distinguish myself from my grandmother, Mary B. Norris, although she had not been known as an actress.) "I'm sorry that you missed the movie of *The Trojan Women*," Hepburn wrote, and I could picture her chin quivering and hear her intonation. "Of course, we played it for laughs. It's the only way – Especially Hecuba –" She signed off, "Good luck and you are certain to be a big hit." It was liberating to know that Hecuba could be outrageous.

Again, Ed Stringham drew on his friends and colleagues to swell the audience. He persuaded Beata to come; a woman who had worked for him back in the sixties—they had studied Greek popular music together—drove down from Rhode Island with her husband. Someone from the managing editor's office came, and even a guy from the makeup department. The office was now in the throes of the takeover by Condé Nast, and this state of emergency may have contributed to the sudden interest in the fall of Troy.

The chorus in this production numbered two; between them, they encompassed all manner of feminine extremes. They were Italy and France, the moon and the evening star, Artemis and Aphrodite. Offstage, they referred to our costumes, flimsy peach-colored shifts, as Burger King uniforms. Hector's shield was molded plastic. So was the prop rock that stood for all Troy: when I leaned on it, the earth moved. My brother, as usual, gave commonsense advice: "Don't waste your time worrying about anything that's not under your control."

The undergraduate who played Helen, an international student from Germany, had long red-gold hair, which she chopped off the week before the performance, so that our Helen looked like a punk rocker. Hecuba loathes Helen. She hurls at her a polysyllabic insult—ὦ κατάπτυστον κάρα—best translated monosyllabically as "You slut!" Refuting the rumor that Paris/Alexandros abducted Helen against her will, Hecuba says, "Who among Spartans heard you scream?" A woman in the audience laughed! (Hepburn would have been proud.) Menelaus told me afterward that he almost went off script and handed Helen over to me—"You were so angry!" During that speech, I felt the last drop of bile leave my liver. I had used up all the hate and bitterness in my system.

Two young boys alternated in the role of the dead Astyanax. One was a Puerto Rican child, a wisp of a boy, who was easy to take into my arms, and he lay limp and sweet on the stage. The other was a solid lad, the eight-year-old son of a classics professor. When I laid him on the stage to deliver my last speech over his lifeless body, he crossed his feet. He did this at every rehearsal. We begged him not to—the director asked him, his father commanded him—but he could not help it. He was afraid I was going to castrate him. The audience tittered. At the last performance, after I laid the boy down, I crossed his feet deliberately, as though this arrangement of limbs were a funeral rite of the Trojans.

In the last scene, Hecuba bids farewell to Troy, a "bastion against barbarians." She utters the lament to end all laments: "ὀτοτοτοῖ!" She tries to throw herself on the burning city, but Talthybius objects and the chorus blocks her. My motivation here had been a puzzle. What in my experience could possibly measure up to that of a queen being banished from her fabled city? My grandmother, in her eighties, had had to leave Cleveland for Clemson, South Carolina, to live with her widowed daughter. That was sad but not tragic.

And then I got it. As *The New Yorker* was being taken over by Condé Nast, I had seen how hard it was for my friend Peter Fleischmann to lose control of the company that his family had built. His father, Raoul Fleischmann, was the original backer of *The New Yorker*, beginning in the 1920s. Peter was proud of the magazine, and of the traditional separation between business and editorial that he had inherited and fostered, and of his relationship with William Shawn. He loved the writers. Peter, like J. D. Salinger, had fought in the Battle of the Bulge, an experience so demoralizing that few of the veterans ever talked about it. After the Liberation he drank champagne in Paris with A. J. Liebling. I loved listening to Peter's stories. He had had throat cancer (he was a heavy smoker), and the surgeons had saved his life but could not save his voice. After that, he was mute unless he used a speaking tube. This gadget was a medical marvel. It looked like an ordinary microphone, but when he pressed it to his throat its vibrations allowed him to say anything he wanted to, albeit in a voice that sounded like a robot's. He called it his tooter. Peter was terse anyway, and could curse with the best of them, so it was especially funny when he picked up his tooter, nestled it against his throat, and uttered one of his favorite phrases: "YOU'RE FUCKING WELL TOLD."

Peter got angry once when I referred to the "sale" of *The New*

*Yorker.* "I did not sell the magazine," he said. "It was taken over." Someone on the board had sold a significant number of shares to the Newhouse family, who had bought still other shares, and suddenly Peter and his loyalists no longer held a majority. He chose to accept the takeover as gracefully as possible. People assumed that, as a businessman, Fleischmann "the yeast magnate" was happy to cash in. But Peter was a principled businessman with a gift for friendship, and he saw it as his duty to make a profit for the shareholders. For Peter the takeover of *The New Yorker* was a profound loss. So that was my farewell to Troy and Peter's to *The New Yorker*, a bastion against barbarians.

At "the last and final terminal end," as Hecuba puts it, in a typical Greek pileup of synonyms, the Trojan women are led to the ships (or, as the program put it, "the chips"; I was not the proofreader for the production), and Hecuba tells the chorus that the only thing they have left is the knowledge that someday their losses will make good stories. "What a bitter speech!" one member of my chorus said when I translated it for her. I thought it was beautiful, a moment of acceptance for Hecuba, a small, cold consolation. But I think I was wrong. Hecuba is like her great enemy Achilles in that she would rather have lived a long, uneventful life and died in obscurity than be immortal in plays and poetry.

When I went back to work the following week, someone at the office asked, "How was the play?" I said, "It was great," and he responded, archly, "If you do say so yourself?" I didn't bother to explain that I didn't mean *I* was great but that the play had been a great experience for me, the best possible therapy. For days afterward, I felt clean and empty. A rival at the office, someone I had formerly wanted to hang by her ankles from the window of the nineteenth floor the way Zeus hung Hera from Olympus (it was her I raged at when I yelled at Helen), was a harmless colleague with pixie ears and a jaunty wardrobe. I had put myself at the service of Euripides, and of Apollo and Dionysus, the gods of theater, and they had accepted my tribute.

CHAPTER 6

# SWIMMING WITH APHRODITE

"WHY WOULD ANYONE want to go to Cyprus?" the man
asked. He was a friend of a friend, and he happened to
be a psychiatrist.

"Because it's the most beautiful place in the world,"
I answered, unhesitatingly. Cyprus was the birthplace of
Aphrodite, goddess of beauty and love and sex and desire—
how could it not be beautiful? And why would anyone not
want to see that? I was fresh back from Greece, at a pool
party in Princeton. The psychiatrist traveled only in August
and preferred guided tours. He had been hot-air ballooning in
the Sahara. If I had been trying to impress him, I would have
washed my feet. I had gotten caught in a downpour the day
before, and the dye from my shoes had turned my feet purple.
But I wasn't, so I jumped into the pool.

Of course, Cyprus *was* a war zone: the Greek and the Turkish Cypriots had been fighting over it since 1963, in what was only the latest skirmish in a long, long history of conflict. In a way, that made it more attractive to me—magnetic, even. Cyprus was the very nexus of war and beauty, conflict and desire. In the words of the Michelin Guide, it was worth a detour—in my case, a seven-hundred-mile Mediterranean detour on the way from Athens to Istanbul.

My relationship with beauty (and love and sex and desire) had always been fraught. I was unable to look in the mirror without finding fault. I had a moon face and a red nose and a double chin and a space between my two front teeth. In makeup I felt like a clown. Cosmetics only emphasize one's natural features, and unless these have some allure to begin with, what is the point? I'd seen the plainest-looking women at the office primping in the ladies'-room mirror, and wondered, Why are they wasting their time?

Beauty requires grooming and bathing. Beauty parlors and dry cleaners are named for Aphrodite (and for her Roman counterpart, Venus). Her name, by folk etymology (which is my favorite kind), means "foam-born"—Hesiod describes how she sprang up from the sea when the detached genitals of Uranus, the original sky god, sickled off by Kronos, hit the water sizzling. But when the goddess of love has risen from her bath, who cleans the tub?

When I poured libations to the gods and tried to cover the

entire pantheon, to get them all on my side—Zeus, Athena, Apollo, Hermes . . .—often I would forget Aphrodite. Sometimes I dared to invoke her when I embarked on a thorough housecleaning. What other goddess might look with favor on the lifelong project of cleanliness? Was Aphrodite the patroness of charwomen? If I had a vexed relationship with beauty and love and sex, it was my own fault for entertaining thoughts like this.

Cleaning is serious business in Greece, thanks to all those crumbling ruins. Housewives are forever sweeping the floor. The Greek word for broom is *skoupa*, and on islands in the Aegean the σκούπα has its own aisle in the *soupermarket*. I had a Greek landlady in Astoria (having moved on from the Italian-American brothers) who saw rain as an occasion to take her broom outside and scrub the sidewalk. Through her and the sound of her infernal sweeping I made the association between brooms and witches. In Homer, Calypso, the nymph who keeps Odysseus on her island for seven years, bathes her captive, and one can imagine her blissfully sweeping out her cave, twirling the broom to make patterns on the earthen floor, as a prelude to seduction and lovemaking.

Many of the labors of Herakles involved cleaning, and his trick was to make it look easy, by, for instance, diverting a stream to muck out the Augean stables. In the aisle of cleaning products, this demigod is represented by a superior-strength brand of clothesline. But it is a mortal who gained worldwide fame as an all-purpose warrior against dirt: Ajax. He does dishes, he does laundry, he removes the bathtub ring—he even does windows. The great hero of the Trojan War resides in a spritzer bottle under the kitchen sink or a can of cleanser behind the toilet. Small wonder that Ajax committed suicide.

The traditional birthplace of Aphrodite is the island of Cythera, off the coast of the Peloponnese. It's not a very big island, and she didn't stick around. Aphrodite needed a bigger stage. She chose Cyprus, or Cyprus chose her. It is a strikingly beautiful island, girdled in blue, with voluptuous rocks and veins of copper. I went there intent on seeing as much as I could in a short time. There were Roman mosaics in Paphos, a city sacred to Aphrodite. There was a cedar tree endemic only to the valley of the Troodos Mountains, and a species of wild sheep called the mouflon. There was a monastery, Stavrovouni, that was overrun with cats (and is said to have a fragment of the True Cross brought from Jerusalem by Saint Helena, Constantine's mother). I hoped to make it to the capital, Nicosia, where the war was most visible; a peacekeeping contingent from the United Nations guarded a buffer zone that cut through the capital, from city gate to city gate, like a jagged blue-and-white scar.

The true border of an island is its coastline, and that's what most interested me in Cyprus: the surrounding sea. I had been to only a handful of beaches—Edgewater, on Lake Erie, of course, the Jersey Shore, Long Island, the Gulf of Mexico at Veracruz. Cyprus promised to have vast stretches of dazzling beauty, with sun twinkling on the water, and foam frilling toward the shore in choreographed lines of scalloped waves. I set my sights on a "beauty spot" that my guide-book said was "by legend the bathing place of the Goddess of Love." It was near a beach, and word was that if you swam out to the rocks at Aphrodite's beach you would be transformed into a beauty for-ever. I wanted to baptize myself in the waters of Aphrodite.

THE *SOL PHRYNE* had come from Venice and was bound for Haifa. I boarded in Rhodes with a deck-class ticket, after get-ting off a ferry from Crete. A backpacking elite—beautiful peo-ple with deep tans and tiny orange bathing suits—had staked out the sundeck: they had pitched tents and strung up clothes-lines and were tossing a Frisbee for their dogs. It was as if the *Sol Phryne* were their personal chartered vessel. My own style of travel combined the spirit of backpacking with the burden of conventional luggage: I traveled light, but I had no sleeping bag or bottled water. Instead I had a striped cotton blanket I'd bought in Crete and a flask of whiskey.

I found a spot on a slatted bench outside the lounge, under an exhaust pipe. I needed to sleep, having stayed up all night on the ferry from Crete to Rhodes, flirting with sailors. The captain had invited me onto the bridge, with its vast array of gauges and gizmos and its unrivaled view of our path through the sea. The chief petty officer, a curly-haired young guy, tried to impress me with his worldliness. "I have been 46 days in Flussing," he said, referring to Flushing, Queens. Once again, I had to explain that I was traveling alone, but I put the accent on the wrong syllable. "Don't say that," the young officer told me. I had said something like "I am a traveling cunt."

He showed me his cabin and was playing with the buttons on my sweater when he was summoned to the bridge by the public address system. Returning to my seat, I fell in with an able-bodied seaman who took me down to the car deck, where we sat in a passenger's Saab and listened to Greek music on the radio. He also showed me his cabin, which was way, way below, and had pinups on the walls and dirty magazines, and there ended—at least, for me—a dry spell. He was in charge of the anchor, so at every port he had to go up on deck and lower away. In the morning I wanted to be on deck again, and that's when I discovered he had locked me in for safekeeping. I tried not to panic—surely he would be back soon. Finally, I managed to jiggle the hook out of the eye from inside and escape, climbing the ladder-like stairs and popping out of the hatch, to the amazement of the captain at his post on the bridge.

On the *Sol Phryne*, wrapped in my Cretan blanket, I dozed off on the slatted bench, and was woken by some young men who were standing on the bench at my feet, reaching through a porthole above me. They pulled out a square, flat package, like a brown paper pillow, and slapped it onto the deck. "Is that yours?" I asked, in Greek. (I wasn't sure whether one addressed a suspected burglar in the formal or the familiar.) "You speak

Greek?" one of the boys asked. "A little," I said, and then demonstrated exactly how little by not understanding what he said next. He translated: "This crazy boy has a snake." He toed the package, and it moved. I reverted to English—primitive English—bellowing "No snake!" as I gathered my belongings and moved.

I found a spot on a lower deck outside a nightclub, where an Israeli youth group was having a party. A band was playing American hits from the early sixties, my pajama-party years: "Let's Lock the Door (And Throw Away the Key)." When the band finally quit, the kids took over, singing and beating tambourines. There was an explosion—my first thought was that someone had shot the snake. But a man who was strolling past had investigated, and he reassured me. "A bomb," he said. Bombs were apparently not unusual on ships in these waters, but on this occasion the *Sol Phryne* did not sink.

At dawn, Cyprus was in sight.

IN THE PORT OF LIMASSOL, on the Greek Cypriot coast, I rented the only car they had left (or so I was told)—a yellow Fiat 500 Mini—and headed for Paphos, forty miles west. I studied the map. Cyprus, solid black, was inset against the white of the Mediterranean, with Europe, Asia, and Africa sketched in. She looked like a witch flying east, the curve of her tall pointy hat following the Turkish coastline, aimed at an inlet that would gladly receive her. Turkey could inhale Cyprus. Although it looked as if the island might have broken off of Turkey, Cyprus was created separately, heaved up from the depths of the sea. The rocks there are unique in the world. Because of its strategic position in the Mediterranean, Cyprus has been occupied by nearly every successive power in the region: the Egyptians, the Greeks, the Phoenicians, the Persians, the Greeks again (Alexander), the Romans, Constantine (the Byzantine Empire), the Crusaders, the French Lusignans, the Venetians, the Ottomans, and the British, until finally, cataclysms later, it became an autonomous state, which then became a battleground of Cypriots, falling into their own nationalist Greek and Turkish camps.

They drive on the left in Cyprus, a legacy of the British. The signs were in Greek and English, sometimes in Turkish, and, near the port, in German, French, and Hebrew. Distances were measured in miles, not kilometers. Gasoline was sold in liters, not gallons. I came of age crossing Pennsylvania on I-80 at seventy miles an hour, so I calculated that I could make it from Limassol to Paphos in less than an hour. I stopped at Ancient Kourion, which had a sanctuary to Apollo and a theater built on a slope with a jaw-dropping view. The Greeks had a genius for knowing where to build. A teenage boy was in charge of the sanctuary. A radio hanging outside the ticket booth was blasting pop music. I would have preferred meditative silence, but Apollo was the god of music; this young man was his proxy, and I was on his turf. I had the sensation, walking on what was left of the temple walls—

low stone dividers between long-gone rooms—that, instead of the ruins' evoking history, I was a ghost haunting the past.

When I got back on the road, the sun was starting to set, and I worried about finding my way to Paphos in the dark. I wasn't sure the headlights were working, so I pulled off the road to check. The road hugged the sea, and what I saw when I turned to get out of the car made me forget about checking the headlights. White rocks studded the water, extending the land into the sea, which was a deep, pure blue, and the road behind me curved along the shore, a black ribbon threaded between low green hills—even the freshly painted white stripe down its middle looked like an adornment. All was still and silent. The place spangled, every element expressing its essence in shape and color: natural beauty meticulously groomed. The place was called Petra tou Romiou, and it was the celebrated birthplace of Cyprian Aphrodite.

The headlights were indeed not working, but I was so enchanted that I could not be too dismayed. I followed the white line as well as I could in the dimming light, and when night dropped its cloak of rich black velvet (hah!) and I found myself inching along a deserted industrial strip, I turned onto a side street and stopped in front of the first house with lights on. The family who lived there came out, and instead of trying to give me directions they all got in their car and escorted me to my hotel, the Dionysus. It had taken me five hours (with the stops to worship Apollo and Aphrodite) to drive forty miles.

After two nights on boats, I luxuriated in the private bath at the Hotel Dionysus. Then I went out for something to eat. Bouzouki music was coming from a restaurant. The bouzouki, or its predecessor the lyre, was said to have been fashioned by Hermes from a tortoiseshell and strung with sheep guts. It has a distinctive twanging sound, more exotic than a guitar. The owner of the restaurant was standing outside, as restaurant barkers do, and invited me in. He was very attentive, offering me an aperitif of Cypriot brandy and serving me a perfect meal: a salad of chopped cabbage and green tomatoes, swordfish souvlaki, French fries, and white wine. Any pub will give you a wedge of lemon with your fish and chips, but this plate came with an entire sliced lemon, which the owner showed me how to squeeze over everything, potatoes and all. Cyprus is rich in lemons.

Also in the restaurant were a few couples from England and Wales, the fisherman who supplied the restaurant (his son was playing the bouzouki), and two swarthy guys who had been out on the fishing boat, one of whom started to flirt with me but was suppressed by the owner.

"How long have you been in Paphos?" the Englishman asked.

"About an hour," I said.

"How long are you staying?"

"I'm leaving in the morning." He and his wife were there for two weeks. I have always been the kind of traveler who has to see everything within a five-hundred-mile radius. I had three days to see as much of Cyprus as possible before getting back to Limassol and catching a boat to Rhodes in time to connect with a smaller boat that left once a week, on Mondays, for ports in the Dodecanese. Maybe someday I would mature into the other kind of traveler, who stays in one place and soaks it up. Not today.

One of the fishermen joined me at my table, over the protests of the owner, and gave me some practice in Greek. Speaking very slowly, as if to a four-year-old, he told me his name was Andreas. I knew the word for "lights"—*phóta*, from *phos* (φως), as in phosphorus, the light-bearing element—and turned out to be quite fluent on the subject of broken headlights. He called over his friend, Grigori, who happened to be a mechanic. They offered to have a look at the car, and if they couldn't fix τα φώτα that night, I could bring the car to Grigori's garage in the morning. I told them I planned to drive to Nicosia, and they corrected me—Greek Cypriots refer to the capital as Lefkosia—and tried to discourage me. Why would anyone want to go to Lefkosia? It was a mess. The Turks, in occupying the north of the island from Morphou to Famagusta, had taken the best lemons. Grigori was from Famagusta, and if he wanted to visit his family he had to go first to Constantinople and then to Ankara to get permission. As a foreigner, I could visit the Turkish sector if I wanted to—Salamis was very beautiful, they said—but I had to be sure and get back before dark. "Why?" I asked. I wanted to get my headlights fixed, in case of emergency, but I did not plan on doing any night driving. "No one saves the bodies," Andreas said.

After dinner, Andreas and Grigori walked me to my car, parked outside the Hotel Dionysus. They determined that the light switch was broken and gave me directions to the garage. I said good night and went into the hotel lobby, which was modern with fluorescent lights glaring off a tiled floor. A man seated in a chair rose up and approached me. It was the restaurant owner. He seemed to think I had agreed to meet him. He was a thin man with dark hair and glittery eyes. Andreas and Grigori had warned me about him. His restaurant was struggling, they said, and his wife had all the money. But what did he want with me? There was no one else in the lobby, no clerk at the reception desk. He took me by the elbow. "One kiss," he said, leaning in. I had heard this before. "One kiss" was what Mimi had said in Crete as he steered me into the cave of the Minotaur. "One kiss" was what the able-bodied seaman had said on the boat from Crete to Rhodes. I knew what "one kiss" meant. It was meant to unlock the whole apparatus. I backed away from him and ran down the hall. As I opened the door to my room, he stood there, arms at his sides, and called imploringly, as if we were breaking up after a torrid affair, "Like this? Like this?"

MEN . . . WHY DID I WANT ONE? *Did* I want one? For the past year, I'd been on a self-improvement kick, hoping to eliminate anything that might prevent me from attracting a man. I was determined to beautify myself from the inside out. I'd made a list of doctors to consult: an otorhinolaryngologist for my ears (*ota*), nose (*rhino*), and throat (*larynx*); a throat doctor who specialized in singers to address my chronic hoarseness; an optometrist, from whom all I wanted was an updated prescription so that I could get new sunglasses for my trip to Greece and from whom instead I got a glaucoma scare and a diagnosis of "convergence deficiency," which basically meant that, as a proofreader, I was in the wrong line of work. The dentist and the gynecologist competed for last and most-dreaded doctor on the list, and the gynecologist won.

The OB-GYN was Greek, which pleased me, though I didn't like his looks. He was short with a square head and bristly black hair. His wife worked with him, while their son, who had his father's bear-bristle hair, did his homework in the waiting room. This was a family weirdly at home in the world of female genitalia.

The word "gynecologist" is from the ancient Greek γυνή, pronounced (in the vocative) "goon-eye." It is what Jerry Lewis would yell in Greek instead of "Hey, lady!" The word has settled into modern Greek as γυναίκα ("yee-*neck*-ah"), a slipperier, more lip-smacking word. Traveling in Greece with this etymological burden, I felt as if Greek men saw nothing of my face or eyes or hair but, like the gynecologist, zoomed in on the goon-eye.

"You will feel a slight pinch," the gynecologist said as he examined me. I sank my teeth into the meaty part of my hand below the thumb. He asked about my "sexual relations" and I told him I had none: I was celibate. (I had a crush on someone who was not interested in me and I was biding my time till I was worthy.) A friend had confided that when she told her gynecologist she was celibate he insisted that she was a lesbian. "He started to ask about birth control," she said, incredulously, "and then stopped himself, saying, 'But you won't need birth control, as you're lesbian.'" Later, in his office, the Greek gynecologist said, "I find you in good health." Then, snapping a rubber band around a brown medicine bottle that contained my cervical cells, he asked inquisitively, "You have no relations?" "Yes," I answered brightly. "I have a brother."

I also had a psychotherapist, to whom I reported this howler. The first diagnosis I ever received from a shrink (you had to have a diagnosis to collect on the insurance) was dysthymia. Unable to find it in the dictionary, I teased it apart by its roots: *dys*, the opposite of *eu*, meant something bad, as in "dystopia," a bad place. For *thymia*, I remembered that in the *Iliad*, when a warrior was defeated in battle, he felt it in his *thymós*. The θυμός was the seat of the passions, which the Greeks located somewhere in the chest. (In English, the gland called the thymus is in the throat.) It means spirit, soul, heart, anger. A diagnosis of dysthymia meant I was downhearted. Was there a cure for that?

The shrink followed my medical adventures with some skepticism. She thought that my ears-nose-throat-voice-eyes-teeth problems were all "displacement," and that what really worried me was my genitalia. I had trouble finding the female body beautiful. We had a running battle in which I maintained that my shame about my body was all my mother's fault. Motor-mouth Mom was one of seven children, six girls and one boy. "He wanted a boy in the worst way, and he kept on getting girls," she would say of her father. "Finally, on the sixth try, he got a boy, and he says to my mother, he says he says he says, 'This one's mine—you take care of the rest.'"

What I absorbed from this, and from the way my mother seemed to favor my brothers, was that a girl was worthless except for helping around the house. We were slaves to Ajax and the *skoupa* and the heraklean clothesline. I was obviously jealous, but I insisted to the shrink that I did not suffer from penis envy. The only thing I envied was the male's ability to pee standing up. Then came a pivotal session. We were talking about hospitals, because my father, in Cleveland, was having surgery for an aortic aneurism. The shrink believed that I was afraid of hospitals because I associated them with being castrated. "But nothing ever happened to my ba—" I was halfway through that last word—balls—when I realized I had misspoken.

"Touché!" the shrink's look said. I had refused to admit to penis envy, that Freudian cliché, but now it seemed I had something worse, a strain of penis envy of cosmic proportions. The shrink had brought me around to seeing that I had somehow cultivated a fantasy that I'd been born male and castrated at birth, a fantasy intended to shore up my worth in my own eyes. I thought all females were mutilated, made wrong, damaged, monstrous.

In mythology, it would be nothing to have someone take a sickle to your balls and scatter your seed all over creation, as Kronos did to Uranus, giving rise to foam-born Aphrodite. But in real life these cases are rare, especially among females. Preposterous as it sounds, the shrink's interpretation explained a lot. Once, I heard my father, coming in out of the cold on a winter night, say to my mother, "I almost froze my balls off." I tried using that expression—I was pretty sure I had balls; they were just round things, right?—and my mother burst out laughing. Another time, I was zipping my pants and my mother mocked me, saying, "You did that just like a boy." She demonstrated by grabbing a wad of fabric at the front of her housedress and zipping up an imaginary fly. Mom was busting my balls.

I went from seeing a psychotherapist once a week to undergoing a full-blown Freudian analysis, fifty minutes a day, five days a week, for years, using up two lifetimes' worth of mental-health benefits from my generous employer. I used to arrive at work with bits of Kleenex stuck to my eyelashes. Gradually, I saw that it wasn't really my mother's fault—she and I had just missed. Sadness was deeper than anger, and under sadness was love. Finally, one spring day, having gone swimming after a Greek class, I was sitting outside on the Columbia campus, balancing my checkbook and eating a hard-boiled egg, and I looked at the name printed on my checks: it was a combination of my grandmother's first name, Mary, and my father's last name, Norris. It was a feminine name, and it was my name (and my money in the bank), and suddenly it came to me that there was nothing wrong with me. I was not a mutilated male but an intact female, like half the human race.

I COULD NOT LEAVE PAPHOS without seeing the Roman mosaics. First thing in the morning, I checked out of the Hotel Dionysus and found my way to the "archaeological park"—a sort of theme park for students of ancient art history. The Romans who lived here two millennia ago paved their floors with stone mosaics, hundreds of small squares of colored stone—tesserae— arranged in scenes from mythology, embellished with vignettes from the natural world. The dig was ongoing, and the archae- ologists were still trying to figure out the best way to display what they had uncovered, without resorting to Plexiglas. Visi- tors stood on a sort of catwalk that formed a grid some three feet above the floors of the homes of the rich and famous in a neighborhood dating to the second century AD, and peered down into their living rooms. The mosaics were dusty but well preserved: stone, if not quite eternal, is a lot more lasting than anything else on the planet. A splash of water would bring out the colors: soft burgundy, warm yellow, creamy white, rich gray, smooth black.

The floors were like tapestries made of stone. There was an astonishing variety of scenes: Theseus, the legendary king of Athens, who slew the Minotaur; Orpheus, the doomed musician, plucking his lyre; Dionysus, the god of booze, sprawled on the back of a leopard, his name spelled out in stones. The Greek letter sigma (Σ) looked like a "C" in ΔIONYCOC. I thought it was Latin, but it's something called a lunate (moonlike) sigma. All the corners were decorated with flowers and animals: oxen, lions, fish, birds, the peacock associated with Hera. The images were framed with different patterns: waves or checks or the Greek key motif.

I had never thought about mosaic art before, but here was something practical (a floor), enduring (stone), beautiful, and orderly (the check pattern may have come from tesserated stone), and it aroused in me what I suppose is a naive response to art: desire. I wanted it. As Samuel Johnson said of Greek and lace, I wanted as much of it as I could get.

I left the mosaics all too soon and reported to the garage where my new friends Andreas and Grigori were waiting to fix my headlights so I could press on in search of Aphrodite and her baths. First we had Cokes; then we had a shot of Finnish vodka; then we had another shot of Finnish vodka ("for the other leg," Andreas said). I protested that I shouldn't drink and drive, but I needn't have worried: I would not be back in the driver's seat for hours. Grigori ordered a new switch for the car. Then he showed me a Citroën that he had totaled and was using for parts. He also had a Jeep, an American model from the thirties, in mint condition. He found a broken red triangle in his toolbox and repaired it. Meanwhile, Andreas pressed me to stay in Paphos: we could all go for a ride in the Jeep, and they would take me fishing. The new switch came, but it had to be converted (whatever that meant). Grigori disappeared, and Andreas, with his thick black hair and lush mustache, plied me with Greek, ever so slowly. He said it was raining in the Troodos, the mountains I would have to drive through to get to Lefkosia. He had never heard of the Baths of Aphrodite. I asked what he was doing that afternoon. I was just curious—surely he didn't spend every day chatting up tourists in his friend's garage—but he thought I was inviting him to come along. So I had to rescind an invitation that I hadn't consciously extended. I told him no one understood why I was traveling alone, and before I could embark on my high-flown feminist ideals he said *"Oúte"*—"Neither do I."

I did not have the facility in Greek to express this to Andreas, but if I hadn't been traveling alone we wouldn't have been talking together like this. When you travel alone, you are forced to engage with people. Otherwise, you're stuck with whatever random song was running in your head when you woke up—the theme from "Mister Ed," say, or "Itsy Bitsy Teenie Weenie Yellow Polkadot Bikini." When you're with someone from home, it is too easy to stay comfortable, in your own idiom and daily regimen and character. You never have the feeling of alienation that is so formative to an experience in a strange place. Living in Greek was a relief from my interior monologue. Because my Greek was limited, I concentrated on saying only things that were direct and essential. There was no place for small talk. Back at home, I was terrible at small talk. In the Mediterranean, no one knew that. I could make myself up as I went along.

If there was a drawback to traveling solo, it was eating alone in restaurants. A single woman needs to be very self-possessed to command a good table in a restaurant. But the upside of that was that I could skip dinner if I wanted and subsist on yogurt and oranges. I could be selfish. I didn't have to consider how my decisions would affect anyone else. I could indulge my penchant for detours. I could slow down if I wanted—and every proposition from a man, like this one from Andreas and Grigori, to skip Aphrodite and go fishing on the sea instead of bathing in it, tempted me. But there was no reason to let anyone keep me from satisfying my own desires. Traveling alone was the only way I knew to go exactly where I wanted to go without having someone try to talk me out of it. I was no one's slave. Life was about my next bed and my next ship and my next city or my next beach. Next! A beautiful word. For heightened pleasure, I would sometimes think of life going on at the office without me, of someone (not me) reading the endless columns of small print. I gloated.

Once in a while the perfect word would come to me spontaneously, and it did so with Andreas in the garage. I told him I was ανυπόμονη (*anypómoni*). Impatient.

When the lights were fixed at last, and I had paid Grigori—the car-rental agency would reimburse me later—and we three had drunk one last coffee together, I gave them both a chaste kiss goodbye and headed north.

It wasn't long before I realized I had left Paphos without getting gas. I now understood that I wasn't traveling on Pennsylvania's I-80, but I still expected to see tall Mobil signs in the distance. In a hilltop village I stopped and used my Greek to ask a man who was walking down the street, "Where can I buy gas?" (I'd practiced.) He got in the car and directed me to the *kafeneion*—the coffeehouse—whose patrons came out to give me directions and ended up forming a phalanx around the car and escorting me, on foot, to the garage, while I drove slowly, as if on parade. Instead of in underground tanks with a pump, the gasoline was stored in cans that came in two sizes, small and large. I picked the large one, the proprietor poured it into my tank, I paid in lira, and the men of the village whose coffee I had interrupted all waved goodbye as I pulled back onto the road.

So far, the only signs of war I had seen were a refugee camp outside Limassol and a lot of poured-concrete buildings under construction to house people relocating from the Turkish sector. An old man with his arm in a sling was hitchhiking in the opposite direction, and I turned around to give him a ride. I felt so rich here in Cyprus, in my little yellow Fiat with its tank full of gas, that I could not pass up an old man who needed a lift. As soon as he got in the car, the old man whipped off the sling—there was nothing wrong with his arm. Back in his village, where I had been tempted to stop anyway, he wanted to buy me a Coke. The *kafeneion* was next to a coppersmith's shop. Cyprus has been famous since antiquity as a source of copper. The coppersmith, surrounded by his family, tried to sell me a round thing with a lid on it. "What is it?" I asked. I couldn't understand the Greek answer, so they translated: "Souvenir." We all laughed. I wanted a souvenir, but if I was going to lug something all over the Mediterranean, it had to serve some practical purpose. This idyll of international trade was interrupted by the arrival of a Cypriot American man in a big flashy car, who silenced the coppersmith's family and demanded to know, in English, how much I paid to rent the Fiat and, when I told him, announced that I had been cheated. I turned back to the copperware and chose a simple ladle with a shallow bowl, the edges of its long handle folded in on themselves. It is in my kitchen, turning green.

BACK ON THE ROAD, eager to get to the Baths of Aphrodite, I followed the map to Polis (City) and turned west along the bay. The baths were supposed to be six miles away, but I had no odometer and could easily misjudge a distance of six miles. Signs started appearing along the road with ambiguous messages like

"Access to Aphrodite's Beach." That might be the one I'd heard of, but the Greeks were full of tricks: a restaurant could call itself the Baths of Aphrodite, post a sign, and lure a tourist miles from the mythical Baths of Aphrodite to their commercial namesake. And I wasn't sure what I was looking for. This beauty spot that my friend Andreas had never heard of—was it an inland pool fed by a waterfall and surrounded by ferns and moss? Or was it a cove along the coast? Which would Aphrodite prefer? She was married to Hephaestus, the lame smith god. Homer tells the story in the *Odyssey* of the time Hephaestus was informed that his wife was carrying on an affair with Ares and devised a net that trapped the lovers in bed together, humiliating them in front of the other gods. Afterward, as Robert Graves puts it in his compendium of Greek myths, Aphrodite had come to Paphos to "renew her virginity." Now, there's a gift. The goddess also had a magic girdle that made everyone fall in love with her. ("Girdle," an ugly word that conjures for me Playtex, must refer to some more flattering garment—perhaps a belt or a sash.)

I could no longer resist the invitations to the Beach of Aphrodite and turned off at one of the signs, which was in fact for a restaurant. It was sparsely populated, and the owner was occupied with a couple at a table. I bought two bottles of beer and escaped down to the beach by myself. There was a group of rocks offshore, some distance away, opposite a cove, and I headed in their direction. The beach was not sandy but sharp with small stones. I passed one couple and didn't meet anyone else till I was almost at the cove of the rocks. A couple there saw me coming and departed—my invisible Gorgon shield on the job. I picked a place among the stones and thistles on the hillside and dumped my blanket and towel, stripped to my bathing suit, and waded into the water.

The best-known image of the goddess of love is Botticelli's *Birth of Venus*, which shows her naked, on a half shell, arms and hair curving over her naughty bits, wafted ashore by a personified breeze. "Laughter-loving" Aphrodite was the original surfer girl. There was no danger of my being confused with her. I paddled out toward the rocks, which were farther away than they looked. This was not the place of ferns described in the guidebook. In fact, it was not in the guidebook. It was through the locals that I had heard of this beach and of the legend that if you swim among the rocks you will be beautiful forever. I was excited and had to calm myself down to swim the distance. This was not a race, after all, but a sensual exercise. What was the rush? I was used to being in a hurry, but I discovered that if I didn't panic I wouldn't run out of breath. The water was warm, the current gentle. No one was watching me. I tried out all my strokes: the dog paddle and the breaststroke and the sidestroke—first on one side, then on the other—and two backstrokes, the one with the frog kick and arms scooping water from underneath and the one with the flutter kick and arms arcing alternately over the head. I ran through the strokes in a series so that I could enjoy the view in every direction. This stroke, which I invented, is called the panoramic. It should be an Olympic event, with the gold medal going to the slowest, most voluptuous swimmer.

I prayed that I was in the right place: O Aphrodite (*breaststroke*), if I have ever neglected to bathe myself and manicure and perfume myself and bedeck myself (*sidestroke left*), if I have scorned to wear the girdle (*backstroke*), I ask you to overlook my flaws and accept this sign of my devotion (*sidestroke right*), honoring air and water (*breaststroke*), sweetness and light (*dolphin dive*). The water was warm and embracing, and the swimming took no effort at all. I sipped at the surface, tasting the salt. I could look back at the beach, with its low mounds of green beyond the shore, and up at the sky, which was cloudy over the mountains (Andreas's warning that it was raining in the Troodos) but clear at the zenith, then out over the glimmer-gray sea to the horizon and ahead to the white rocks. They were a peeled white, like skin treated at a spa, and, close up, they were very suggestive. In the biggest one, I made out the figure of a woman with rounded limbs and full breasts bending over the water. When I reached her, I realized that the best part of her was submerged, a mossy shelf pricked all over with tiny mollusks. I hauled myself onto her lap for a rest. I could not believe it: I had reached the Rocks of Aphrodite, and it was as if all Cyprus belonged to me.

As long as no one was looking, I was tempted to take off my bathing suit. I had skinny-dipped only once before, in a pond in New Jersey, and it felt so daring: my heart had pounded as I got in deep enough to lose foot contact and begin to tread water; I had expected any second to hear a bullhorn and have the police roar into the water in an amphibious squad car and fish me out and book me for indecent exposure. To be naked in the elements—it can only be bad if someone disapproves, as when Yahweh (I-am-who-am) spotted Adam and Eve after the apple in the Garden of Eden. But I was strongly tempted. If a swim around the Rocks of Aphrodite was supposed to make me beautiful, the water had to touch all of me. I wouldn't want to make the mistake of silver-footed Thetis, who held her son Achilles by the heel as she dipped him in the River Styx, leaving that one part of him vulnerable.

Reader, I stripped there on the rock and lowered myself back into the sea. Every nerve fiber was alive as I hovered in the water; there was no layer of Lycra between the sea and me. I clamped the suit between my teeth by its straps and paddled around the rocks like a retriever. I felt as if I had shed a woolen overcoat. The current pushed me gently back to shore and I washed up onto mounds of bleached seaweed, as cushiony as confetti. I felt reborn.

I ate my lunch on the beach—a cheese sandwich left over from breakfast, dried figs, a few cookies, prolonged by the beer, from which I poured generous libations to Aphrodite. I wished now that there were a man with me—someone to enjoy this with—but I had no regrets. Like the island of Cyprus itself, I wanted self-determination. My two wishes might conflict—it seemed impossible to have both love and independence at the same time—but it was liberating to admit I wanted them. And if I had been traveling with someone else I would never have ended up in this place.

I walked back to the car, saturated with beauty. Many tiny burrs stuck to my Cretan blanket. There was a dirt road winding along the hillside, so I could avoid hobbling over those sharp stones. For once, I let myself do something the easy way. I don't know if anyone would say I was changed, but everything I saw was transformed. It was as if I were drugged. Colors of rocks, flowers, pebbles, grass, thistles, sea, cypresses and cedars—all were heightened in beauty and somehow graspable, more palpably there. After being in the sea, I was returning to my own element, to land, and I saw it all anew. I was a long way from home, where I had stood in front of the bathroom mirror with the Ajax and muttered, "Hideouser and hideouser." When I got back to the car, I did something I hadn't done in years: turned the rearview mirror toward me and rearranged my hair.

# CHAPTER 7

# ACROPOLIS NOW

I T  M U S T  B E  said that I was not raised with the highest stan-
dard of beauty. Lake Erie was not beautiful. It was the first
body of water I was ever sat down by, and I remember that the
shore was covered with green slime. I loved the fireworks over
Edgewater Beach one Fourth of July when I was small enough
to ride on my father's shoulders: tiny golden fish clustered into
the shape of one giant fish, a school of fish shaped like a fish
flashing in the night sky. I have never seen fireworks to match.
I did not live in a beautiful place until I moved to Vermont and
had a view of the Adirondacks and a lush green drive to work.
New York always looks beautiful to me when I am leaving it.
Maybe that's the way of it: things are at their most beautiful
when you think you're seeing them for the last time.

So how did I ever develop a taste for Greece?

Nothing was quite what I expected. The light, the famous light, was not brighter than light anywhere else but softer, more delicate, like cream instead of milk, or real maple syrup tasted for the first time. There were no sharp edges but, rather, bands of color along the horizon, shades of distance, whitewashed walls, blue domes, the soft terra-cotta red of roof tiles. The landscape was the setting for the temples: the man-made enhanced the natural and nature set off the man-made. It was the perfect assemblage of elements.

Wherever I went, I heard parents calling to children, "Έλα! Έλα εδώ!" "Come! Come here!" Imagine being a child in Greece, growing up in that landscape, being plopped down on a beach in your ancestral land, learning the word for the sea: θάλασσα (*thálassa*), with the stress on the first syllable, like a wave that breaks and then retreats, hissing, and is overtaken by the next wave, and the next. Once, walking down a hillside to the sea, admiring a terraced garden among small pines, I watched as a man removed a block of wood in an ingenious network of irrigation channels, sending the water in a new direction. "Έξυπνος," I said. *Ex + hypnos*—"out from sleep"—is the Greek for smart, intelligent, alert, woke. He smiled. He hadn't invented the system. His ancestors had figured it out millennia ago.

Ed Stringham had spoken appreciatively of Vouliagmeni, a beach outside Athens, but when he traveled, it was for the cities, for the art and culture. "You *must* go to the Benaki," Ed had said. With its rank upon rank of icons and its collections of sculpture, pottery, jewelry, silver—from the archaic to the modern—the Benaki is a world-class museum. Ed impressed on me the importance of the Byzantine in Greek history: the country had missed the Renaissance, he said—it was under the Ottoman Empire while its own ancient glories were being rediscovered in Italy, and it was largely the Orthodox Church that kept Greek culture alive. Although Ed had stressed that Greece looked east, to Asia, rather than west, to the rest of Europe, it was the Parthenon, the symbol of Western civilization, that he spoke about most rhapsodically. He had climbed the Acropolis one night with a poet to view the Parthenon under the full moon. The memory of it made him swoon: the glow of the marble, the shape of the columns against the sky, the poignancy of ruins that were both tragic and triumphant. Seeing the Parthenon had clearly been a highlight of Ed's youth, his "bloom," as the ancients called that epoch of young manhood when a boy is at his most godly. Although it was the landscape and language of Greece that first drew me, Ed's praise made me long to see the Parthenon. Surely it was something that nobody could ever feel jaded about.

So in 1983, on my first day in Athens, right after breakfast, at which I had asked a street vendor for a donkey (*γαϊδούρι*) instead of a yogurt (*γιαούρτι*)—not even close—I went straight to the Acropolis. I was sitting on a big rock by the stairs to the Parthenon when a man who looked Greek addressed me in German, inviting me to join him and his friends. The German threw me off—I didn't come to Greece to speak German. I declined, and he said, in Greek, "You don't want to?" He was Greek after all. Only later did I realize that he had addressed me in German because he thought *I* was German—that was the default nationality of fair-skinned women traveling in Greece. Americans were rarer, and even rarer was the fair-skinned American who didn't get it when a Greek was trying to pick her up.

"Acropolis" means "the upper fortified part or citadel of a Greek city," "a place of refuge." In ancient times, people protected themselves by gathering together on a height where they could see enemies approaching and roll rocks down on them. Whoever is up high has an advantage. "Refuge" as a definition has developed from the function of the place, but its literal meaning—from *akro*, edge, and *polis*, city—is the Upper City, the Heights. Although the English word acrophobia (*akro* + *phobia*) is a fear of heights, *akro* can also mean edge. An acrophobic may not mind being in a high place as long as he doesn't have to look over the edge. Athens is a hilly city—not an easy place to ride a bicycle—but, compared with the mountains in the east and north, it slopes like a plain to the sea in the west and south. The Acropolis is a mountain peak that somehow got separated from its range and now stands flat-topped in the middle of the city that grew up around it, inspired by it, depending on it for refuge.

The city of Akron in northeastern Ohio, famous for rubber, tires, and the Goodyear blimp, takes its name from the Greek *akro*. I went there once in high school, and by Ohio standards it did feel rather elevated. Akron sits on a western plateau of the Alleghenies, 1,004 feet above sea level; the Acropolis in Athens is 490 feet above sea level, but it is not part of a plateau. It's a high, sharp rock that juts up out of the chaotic city like a huge shard.

On that trip, my view of the Parthenon, the temple to Athena the Virgin that crowns the Acropolis, was compromised by scaffolding and rusty-looking machinery. It was like going to Venice when the Campanile is under renovation or the Alhambra when the fountain in the Court of the Lions is being replumbed. It was disappointing. All I could do was try to get a grip on the history of the Parthenon. A less grand version begun by the Athenians after the Battle of Marathon, in 490 BC, was destroyed by the Persians and then reconstructed, more grandly, under Pericles in 447 BC. Construction took nine years, and it stood until 1687, when it was blown up by the Venetians, who shot mortars at it when they learned (from the Greeks) that the Ottomans were using it as a weapons depot. By 1983, the Parthenon had been a ruin for three hundred years—ten generations. What was the likelihood that it would be restored during my lifetime?

I wandered around with my Blue Guide, but it was hard to match what I was supposed to be seeing with what was actually there. I didn't know the archaeological terms—metopes, naos, propylaea. There was a pocket museum right there on the Acropolis, and I saw the damage the pollution had done to the sculptures, eating away the marble. Personally, I was not sensitive to the bad air—the Cloud, as the Athenians called the smog created by traffic emissions. Cleveland is a steel town, and New Jersey has a petrochemical refinery or two. To me the air of Athens smelled piney, like retsina. But the decay of the stone was tragic.

The next time I climbed the Acropolis was in 1985. I arrived in Athens via London, where I visited the British Museum to see the Elgin Marbles. I bought postcards and books and learned to recognize Herakles by his lion skin and Hermes by his floppy hat and winged sandals. There was a lot of fighting going on in the friezes: battles of Centaurs, Lapiths, Amazons. Centaurs, of course, had the bodies of horses and the heads and torsos of men. Lapiths were mythological beings from Thessaly, who mostly fought with Centaurs. The Amazons were a mythical tribe of warrior women who scheduled conjugal visits with the opposite sex once a year, strictly for procreation. They excelled at archery, and legend has it that a girl's right breast was cauterized so that she would grow up better equipped to shoot arrows. (The name Amazon is supposedly from *a-mazos*, without a breast.) In our time the word Amazon is more likely to be associated with the empire of Jeff Bezos and online shopping for books and for bows and arrows—and for bras and prostheses, for that matter. The behemoth company was named for the Amazon River, which was named for the Amazons.

There were a lot of animals in the sculptures—a wide-eyed ox being led to sacrifice, horses whinnying—and young girls in the Panathenaic procession carrying pomegranates and gifts for the goddess. The most beautiful sculptures from the Acropolis, to me, were the Caryatids: strong, graceful female figures supporting the porch roof of the small temple called the Erechtheion. (I am always embarrassed to pronounce the word, but I'm told it's *carr*-y-a-tids.) Lord Elgin's men took one of them to London, sawing her off the porch and stacking rubble in her place. Lord Byron, a contemporary, deplored his countryman's rape of the Acropolis. The British say that Lord Elgin's action, which took place while he was ambassador to the Ottoman Empire (1799–1803), saved the precious marbles from certain destruction—they would have been neglected under the Ottomans and eroded by pollution in modern times—and make the point that in the British Museum you get to see the figures from the friezes and the pediments up close. The original sculptures were very high on the temple, and even the ancients couldn't have been able to see them very well. But the six Caryatids were rhythmic in their poses, and breaking them up was a sacrilege.

In Athens I climbed the Acropolis again and tried to reassemble it all mentally, but the Parthenon was in fragments and the fragments were scattered all over Europe. Its fragmentation was part of its history now. Even if I lived to be a hundred and fifty and could still scramble up to the heights of the city or command a sedan chair, it was unlikely that I would ever see the Parthenon free of scaffolding, with Doric columns intact and monumental marble gods on the pediments. I would never be able to enter the temple that once housed a colossal statue of Athena and feel the proportions of the place and crane my neck to look at the friezes. The Parthenon of the present was a forlorn reminder of the Parthenon of the past.

AND THEN, INCREDIBLY, just a few years later, it happened. The great bronze doors, richly worked, stood open, and I entered the Parthenon. The temple had a coffered ceiling, and all the sculptures on the metopes, pediments, and friezes had been restored in fine detail. The space was vast, dominated by the huge chryselephantine statue of Athena Parthenos by Phidias, rising more than forty feet tall. And I wasn't dreaming! But I wasn't in Athens, either. I was in Nashville, Tennessee.

At first, I didn't know what to make of the Nashville Parthenon. I thought it was a joke. But, if so, why wasn't everyone there shrieking with laughter? I tried to share the joke with the guard at the temple door, but he seemed to honestly believe that this replica Parthenon was better than the original, because it had all its parts and wasn't crumbling, like the one in Athens. "Look," he said, swinging one of the doors closed. "The doors work." I was incredulous. Had no one noticed that the Parthenon in Athens is on top of a hill and this one was on flat land, surrounded by grass? Where were the rocks? Where was the sense of something built on a sacred height, the shape of the temple cut out against an azure sky? Instead of spotting it in the distance on your way into the city, you roll past it and do a double take. It reminded me of the time I saw the White House through the car window: instead of an awe-inspiring landmark of democracy, it was a long, low dwelling with a wide front lawn.

At a wonderful bookstore aptly called Parnassus I met a woman named F. Lynne Bachleda. "You have to see our Parthenon in context," she said. Nashville calls itself the Athens of the South, and it is full of colleges and universities—a locus of learning, like Athens, Greece. The Greek key motif is worked into the public library (architect, Robert A. M. Stern). (A library is, in fact, sometimes called an athenaeum, after Athena.) The city first constructed a plaster replica of the Parthenon in 1897, for the hundredth anniversary of the state's entry into the Union (1796). It was one of several structures, including a pyramid and a Ferris wheel, that, Lynne said, were "meant to bring foreign cultures, and fun, to Nashville, showing the marvels of the age." The exhibition was like the 1851 Great Exhibition in Victorian London, or the New York World's Fair of 1964. "Our Parthenon has value," Lynne said. "It speaks well of Nashville that we wanted it here." She went on, eloquently, "It is the only place on earth where you can experience the architectural volumes and visual balance of the original, albeit with a very different 'vibe.'"

As a kid in the fifties, Lynne loved going to Centennial Park. There was a lake with ducks and a sunken garden and a fighter plane and a steam locomotive. Lynne's father was a Latin teacher who had also studied Greek, so the family had a classical bent—their dog was a boxer named Psyche. Schoolchildren put coins in a collection box inside the temple to raise money for a statue of Athena. By 1982, thirty years later, they had enough cash to go ahead with the project. A local sculptor named Alan LeQuire won the commission, and a friend of Lynne's, Annie Freeman, posed for the statue. "She had a beautiful strength to her physique, a real grounded strength to her," Lynne said. Annie, an artist and songwriter, was in awe of LeQuire. Sculpting the Athena, she said, was "like trying to replicate the Statue of Liberty from a souvenir."

The best description we have of the monumental statue of Athena was written by Pausanias, in the mid-second century AD. "The statue is made of ivory and gold," he wrote (in Peter Levi's translation). "She has a sphinx on the middle of her helmet, and griffins worked on either side of it. . . . [T]he statue of Athene stands upright in an ankle-length tunic with the head of Medusa carved in ivory on her breast. She has a Victory about eight feet high, and a spear in her hand and a shield at her feet, and a snake beside the shield; this snake might be Erichthonios"—the man-serpent, sprung from the seed of Hephaestus, who is the mythological ancestor of the Athenians.

LeQuire took eight years to complete the statue. He started by researching construction materials and then did historical research, contacting eminent classical archaeologists, like Brunilde Sismondo Ridgway, of Bryn Mawr College, who had written several books on Greek sculpture of the archaic and Hellenistic periods. Rather than regarding the Nashville Athena as a folly, Ridgway chose to see it as a great opportunity to understand how Phidias built the original statue, around 450 BC. LeQuire went to Athens, of course, and measured the base of the place where the Phidias Athena had stood. He also studied a small Roman replica of the Phidias known as the Varvakeion Athena, from the third century AD, in the National Archaeological Museum in Athens. He drove around the Peloponnese, visiting sites associated with Athena, hoping she would appear to him. In a way, he was trying to apprentice himself to Phidias across the ages. He particularly admired the naturalistic poses and drapery of the Caryatids, on the Acropolis. A fifth-century BC head of a woman in Pentelic marble, which he saw in Brescia, Italy, and which might have been by Phidias, gave him the idea for Athena's head.

To make sure that the replica Parthenon could bear the weight of the monumental statue, builders cast four gigantic concrete pylons that went down to Nashville's limestone bedrock. Athena is four stories tall. She is built on a steel armature, clad in panels of gypsum cement reinforced with chopped fiberglass. "The work went on behind a curtain," Lynne recalled, so that when the statue was done, in 1990, it was "more of a magical reveal." The head is oversized, because otherwise, from below, Athena would look like a pinhead. She is so big that the Nike she is holding—the winged goddess of victory, at six feet tall—is to her the size of a basketball trophy. When you stand at her feet, that is what you see: monumental toes. Annie Freeman is modest about having posed for the biggest indoor statue in the world, and quick to give credit to other models. LeQuire is said to have used the feet of another woman to get the toes right. "Those are not my breasts, I can tell you," Annie said. She likes to think that something of her stance and energy went into the statue, along with her nose ("I don't have a pixie nose"), and was gratified when the sculptor told her that he chose her for her "strength of character." Athena's lips are modeled on Elvis Presley's.

Lynne has been to Athens and seen the original Parthenon. "That was frankly disappointing," she said. "You can only get so close. As someone who was raised with being able to walk into it—there's an undeniable advantage to being able to appreciate the proportions of the building." The erudite guide who took her around the Acropolis was not impressed when Lynne told her about the replica of the Parthenon back home. In fact, Lynne said, "She looked at me like I was a turd in a punch bowl." Lynne's favorite view of the Parthenon is from across Lake Watauga, in Centennial Park, when the doors of the temple are open and you can see inside to the gigantic statue. "There's this huge woman, perceiving, assessing, inspiring," she said. "To see her from a distance in statuesque majesty . . . Here is a woman with far-reaching power and the tools of war."

In recent years, the statue has been gilded. "I miss the naked simplicity of the form," Lynne said. "The gilding looks kind of cheesy, to my modern eyes, but I am all for historical accuracy."

The sculptor liked it white, too, but he recognizes that the whiteness of the Parthenon has nothing to do with the Greek aesthetic. "They used as many different materials as they could get their hands on," LeQuire said.

I find the Nashville Athena terrifying, with her helmet and aegis and spear. Her face, since the gilding, is made up with lipstick and eyeliner. This is no mild Mother Mary. But the Nashvillians made a convert of me. Sculpture is one of the so-called plastic arts: it is all about shape. True, there is no substitute for Pentelic marble, for the original stones. That is why the argument between the Greeks and the British over the Elgin Marbles is so bitter. The City College of New York has a set of Parthenon friezes—plaster casts from molds of the originals in the British Museum—on display at the CUNY Graduate Center on Fifth Avenue and Thirty-fourth Street. As shapes, sculptures can be appreciated, at some level, even if they're made of marshmallows. Recently I was delighted to see a mesh screen printed with the image of the Parthenon draping the side of a parking garage in Chicago's Greektown.

I was a snob about the Nashville Parthenon not being up high, but that means a person who uses a wheelchair or someone pushing a baby stroller can go inside. It's within driving distance of Cincinnati. And it's not tacky—it's not an ersatz Las Vegas attraction or any kind of commercial enterprise, like the seedy hotel with an Eiffel Tower on top that you can see from the Brooklyn-Queens Expressway. This Parthenon is not fake but sincere. I would lay a tribute at the feet of the Nashville Athena.

⌾⌾

IN THE SPRING OF 2013, I was invited on a press trip to Athens organized by the Greek Ministry of Culture and Sports to generate advance publicity for an exhibition of Byzantine masterpieces from Greek collections, which would be mounted at the National Gallery in Washington, DC, and at the Getty Museum in Los Angeles. Contemporary Greece was in a financial depression that threatened its membership in the Eurozone. The *New York Times* ran front-page articles about children being sent to school hungry and people scavenging for food in dumpsters. The national airline, Olympic, was no longer operating between New York and Athens. I had to fly an Austrian airline to Vienna and then to Thessaloniki, the second city of Greece—kind of like Chicago—and finally on to Athens. I missed being with Greeks on their own airline: the passengers always gave the pilot a round of applause when the wheels hit the tarmac.

Two young diplomats from Greece's foreign press office were shepherding us on the tour. Both were named Andreas; one was posted to Istanbul, the other to Lisbon, and they were known to their colleagues as the Turk and the Portagee. I asked Andreas the Portagee where he had learned Portuguese, and he said that he had studied at the Ionian University, in Corfu.

I told him that my favorite teacher had taught in the translation program there—Dorothy Gregory. "You knew Dorothy Gregory?" he said, astonished. "I studied with her on Corfu!" We stared at each other, openmouthed. Dorothy—Dora, as she was called in Greece—had died in Corfu in March of 2000, just before I was scheduled to visit. It was wonderful to resurrect her between us. "It is so touching that you knew Mrs. Gregory," Andreas said.

When we checked in at our four-star hotel, I dotted the "i" in my name with such zeal that the pen popped apart in the lobby. I had been a little worried about traveling with a press crew until I saw my room. Because we were guests of the state, we had fabulous accommodations—my room had a balcony and a view of the Acropolis. I had binoculars with me, and whenever I was free I trained them on the rock, watching the way the shadows shifted. I might never have left the hotel. It was in the center of town, a district of Athens that I was unfamiliar with. I usually gravitated toward the Plaka, the slab of the city beneath the Acropolis, and stayed in small two-star hotels on its south side. This place was an art gallery unto itself, and a drink in the rooftop bar, where the view wrapped around to Mount Lycabettus—Athens' other dramatic hill, calling across to the Acropolis—was a decadent experience, all flashing lights, like being at Studio 54 at the height of the disco craze. As I sipped my ouzo, I found myself thinking, I could get used to this. But it was an odd time to be treated like a rich person. On the streets there were angry demonstrations by the Greeks, protesting the austerity regime that the government had imposed to keep the country afloat in the Eurozone. People were facing the fact that they had been getting robbed by corrupt politicians for generations.

We went to the Benaki Museum, which I had visited on earlier trips on Ed's recommendation, and which was sending some of its most precious holdings to the United States as part of the Byzantine exhibit. A curator showed us a mosaic icon of the Virgin, dating to the ninth or tenth century, from Stoudios Monastery in Constantinople. Icons, of course, are a staple of the Greek Orthodox Church, and there are very strict guidelines for icon painters. St. Luke is said to have painted the historical Mary, the Theotokos (God's birth-giver), from life. This piece was unique, a survivor. For one thing, it was stone, not painted wood, and it hadn't shattered. The Virgin's face is beautiful and expressive, with a small mouth, long nose, asymmetrical eyes, and smooth brow; her veil is outlined in dark gray, and the shape of her head is echoed in rings of gold and green-blue: a halo of polychromatic stones. The alphabet book that I bought that day at the Benaki uses the image to illustrate the letter psi (Ψ) for ψηφιδωτό (psephidotó), which it defines as "painting with small colored stones or pebbles." I was surprised to find that there was another Greek word, a technical one, for "mosaic." Greek also uses *mosaicó* (μωσαϊκό), a word I always associated with Moses, as if he had been responsible for putting something precious together from a lot of small parts. But "mosaic" is also related to the Muses and refers to something that has been given an artistic treatment and is worthy of a museum.

We saw beautiful things at the Benaki—classical statues with Christian interpretations, like a stone shepherd carrying a lamb across his shoulders. In the Orthodox view, the Greeks did not miss the Renaissance, as Ed had said, but made the Renaissance possible by bridging the classical and the Christian during the many centuries of the Byzantine Empire. Across the avenue from the Benaki, the Byzantine and Christian Museum, a low sand-colored building, like a mission church in California, is devoted to this theme. It was lending the exhibition a thirteenth-century mosaic icon of the Madonna and Child called the Virgin Episkepsis (the Sheltering Virgin or the Virgin of Tenderness); the literal meaning of the epithet is "looking over," as in "watching out for." The Virgin's features are the same as in the mosaic icon at the Benaki: small mouth, long nose, sad eyes. The face, contoured by the colored stones, has a delicate suggestion of rose in the cheeks. Her veil is framed in deep blue and striped with gold. It occurred to me that the halo might be an artifact of the mosaic process: the repeated outline creates an aura around the head. The icon has visible seams running lengthwise, along which it has lost some of its tiles, and appears to have been assembled in thirds. It arrived in mainland Greece from Tirilye in 1922, the year the Turks ejected the Greeks from Asia Minor, slaughtering people who had lived there for generations, burning Smyrna, and putting an end to the Great Idea, the notion that Greece would one day take back Constantinople and Asia Minor. Greeks call it the Catastrophe. Even disfigured, the Virgin of Tenderness was a supreme example of mosaic art.

Ever since I saw the mosaics at Paphos, on Cyprus, and was denied entry to the monastery at Dafni, I have gone out of my way to view mosaics wherever I can. There are Roman mosaics in Fishbourne, in the south of England. Rome itself has several jewel-like Byzantine churches, including Santa Maria in Cosmedin (home of the Bocca della Verità, supposedly the head of Uranus, whose open mouth is said to close on the hand of anyone not telling the truth—an early lie detector). Venice showcases the exquisite work of mosaic artists imported from Constantinople by the doges. I particularly love the floors (*pavimenti*) of St. Mark's Basilica and of churches on Torcello and Murano, with their swirling patterns of concentric circles made of triangular chips of gray and white and golden stone, or simple colored squares—deep blue, burgundy, green—locked together and polished smooth. Their cool beauty makes me want to prostrate myself, if only to get closer to the stone.

I had been to Pompeii, Herculaneum, and Paestum, all near Napoli, which started out as a Greek colony; spent a week in Ravenna, an outpost of Byzantium (and Dante's place of exile); and driven into Palermo (hair-raising), where on entering the Palatine Chapel I murmured to my companion, "I'm in Paradise," to which he responded that this was exactly the effect the creators were striving for: a church should feel like Paradise. But

I had yet to see the Holy Grail of Byzantine mosaics: the monastery at Dafni.

Dafni had been on the itinerary of our press tour and then disappeared, a disturbing turn of events, confirmed by the minister of culture himself: "There is some problem with Dafni," he said. The restoration was ongoing. But one of our diplomat shepherds, Andreas the Turk, had always loved Dafni and was moved that an American even knew about it, so he called an archaeologist friend. On a side trip to visit the last strongholds of Byzantium in the Peloponnese, our bus pulled off the Sacred Way fourteen miles outside Athens and stopped at the park in Dafni. I couldn't believe it.

Children suspended their play to watch as the foreign journalists were met at the door and welcomed inside the church. The scaffolding inside made it look like a trapeze school. Finally I understood that it wasn't just for safety reasons that the church had been closed—by now multiple earthquakes had shattered the mosaics, which had collapsed onto the floor in jumbles of tesserae. The restorers' work was of a magnitude I could barely comprehend: they were putting the Almighty together again. The mosaics, in various states of restoration, glowed from the walls and the vaulted ceiling. There was a Nativity scene with sheep and shepherds; a Baptism of Christ, with wavy lines to indicate water over his lower body, immersed in the River Jordan; a Last Supper, the Apostles crowded together around the Redeemer; and a Transfiguration. We were invited to ascend the scaffolding into the dome. Short strings dangled from some of the tiles—a scientific test for humidity or stability—which did not detract one iota from the magnificent impression.

Patrick Leigh Fermor, who had been here before the earthquakes and seen it whole, wrote in his book *Mani* about "the stupendous mosaic of Christ Pantocrator at Daphni in Attica": "whose great eyes, dark and exorbitant and cast almost furtively over one shoulder, at total variance with His right hand's serene gesture of blessing and admonition, spell not pain but fear, anguish and guilt, as though He were in flight from an appalling doom. The only fit setting for such an expression is the Garden of Gethsemane; but this is a Christ-God in His glory, the All Powerful One. It is tremendous, tragic, mysterious and shattering." I was standing within inches of the Christ Pantocrator, beneath his right hand.

If my travels had a moment to compare to Ed Stringham's experience of the Parthenon, this was it. My gratitude has made me easier to get along with ever since. Back in Athens, I was more than content to join my fellow-travelers for a sunset tour of the Acropolis—the kind of thing that really galls you when you are among hoi polloi (Greek for "the many") and see privileged individuals admitted after hours. We were an eccentric bunch: an ambitious freelancer, keen to solidify her relationships with the Ministry of Culture; a gentlemanly Southern wine writer; an art snob from the Upper East Side; a fresh young Mormon woman who worked in radio and lugged her equipment up the

Acropolis, unsheathing a microphone the size of a giant zucchini. She refused wine at meals but drank in Greece with bottomless delight, reminding me of my younger self. As she hovered near our guide, a young man in khaki shorts and work shirt, with her giant padded microphone, we draped ourselves over the smooth rocks and listened. The guide talked about the restoration efforts, which entailed undoing the misguided restoration efforts of earlier generations. A young reporter from the West Coast took notes in a whimsical notebook with a purple pen—I imagined her dotting her "i"s with daisies and marveled at how easy and feminine she made it look to be a writer.

When we had wandered around for a while and it was time to leave, the West Coast writer discovered that she had lost her pen. "It's my favorite pen!" she cried, and it was clear that the Acropolis would not be closing for the night until she had found it. We fanned out over the rocks, some of us more optimistic and willing than others, to make our fellow writer happy. I concentrated on the spot where I had watched her dotting her "i"s, her dark hair framing her lovely face, her short skirt belling around her. She was married with a young daughter and hadn't been lucky so far on this trip, missing her connection in Vienna, oversleeping in the morning, passing out early in the evening. She would later confirm what I had suspected: she was pregnant. As a pencil lover, I understood the attachment to a writing tool—I was traveling with a quiver of Blackwings. Looking down, I spotted the pen hiding in a crevice of the rock, and said casually, "I

found it," instantly regretting that I had not nabbed this opportunity to shout in Greek, "Εύρηκα!" I found it! Eureka!

SOMEHOW WHEN A CITY IS ANCIENT you don't expect
it to change that much, but Greater Athens is a dynamic megalopolis. In recent years it hosted the Summer Olympics and
built a new airport, got gleaming new Metro lines up and running, and opened the new Acropolis Museum. This is on the
south side of the Acropolis, set back from a promenade planted
with rosemary and thyme. A broad entrance ramp gives visitors
a chance to look down at the archaeological site through green-
tinged glass. Inside, findings from the Acropolis are arranged
behind glass on both sides of a long corridor. The museum is
built on several stories, with the sculptures installed at the level
on which they would be found if they were still attached to the
temple. A visitor can enjoy the details of metopes and friezes,
in natural light, while looking out the floor-to-ceiling windows
at the Acropolis itself. The Caryatids have been moved inside
to protect them from the pollution, so you can see them up
close, admire their thick hair in its intricate braids, and peek
out from behind them as if you were with them on the porch of
the Erechtheion. (The ones on the Acropolis are reproductions.)
The Greeks have left poignant blanks for the marble gods and
doomed oxen and whinnying horses that reside in London.

The last time I was in Athens, in the spring of 2017, with no fancy press credentials, I went again to the Acropolis. I tried to get there early, before it got too crowded, but by the time I arrived at the ticket booth it was 10:15. The day was already hot, and the Acropolis was thronged. I joined the crowd of people jostling up the stone stairs, worn smooth to gleaming by the feet of supplicants since the time of Pericles. Four Japanese women wearing hats suitable for a garden party linked arms and pushed through the crowd, giggling. A man directed me to move so that he could photograph his wife: no photobombing allowed. Signs that said "Do Not Touch the Marble" made even the most reverent visitor want to reach out and stroke the cool pink stone. As at Dafni, the restoration was ongoing—there were more work crews on scaffolding than I had ever seen on the Parthenon before. Inside the temple, square white umbrellas cast patches of shade for the workers. There was the sound of drills. Column drums and slabs and disks, organized by size and shape, were lined up and labeled: a library of fragments. There was a railroad up there, and cranes and pulleys and tractors and carts full of stones. Minus the modern technology, it must have looked something like this during the original construction. I thought of a passage from Plutarch that Ed had once left on my desk: a retired mule, after years of labor on the Acropolis, showed up every day to cheer on the younger mules.

The crowd and the scaffolding on the Acropolis didn't bother me this time; the modern trappings did not feel like a barrier between Athena and me. I sought out the olive tree that grows on the Acropolis, descended from the tree said to have been planted by the goddess. Detaching myself from the crowd, I stood in a wedge of shade and looked through a window to a kind of pantry for the workers: a clean white room with a bare table, a bench, a stove, a refrigerator, a sink with gooseneck faucets, a hook to hang a jacket on—nothing extra. It was as if I were looking at Athena's kitchen.

I'm not acrophobic, and I enjoyed looking over the edge and out at the megalopolis (*megalo* + *polis* = big city), the buildings nudging up the mountains and flowing down to the sea. The apartment buildings were all roughly the same size and style: six to eight stories, utilitarian, if not brutalist, with white or pastel facades gridded with balconies divided by panels and rigged with awnings and shades; compact solar-powered hot-water heaters lay on the roofs like blue hippos; and the whole mess bristled with TV antennas. It looked as if the great city had been rendered in impasto, caked with layers of white that had built up over the years like plaque, the whole land a sculpture.

On the way down from the Acropolis that morning, a young woman suffered a laughing fit so infectious that it set off the group she was with and started the whole crowd laughing. My knees went weak as I shuffled down the stairs with the crowd, and if I reached out and touched the marble it was out of necessity, to keep my balance. It suddenly struck me as wonderful that throngs of people come from all over the world every day to climb the Acropolis of Athens and visit the temple of Athena Parthenos, and that Athenians, using the best scientific methods, are at work in their city constantly, industriously, sorting the ruins and shoring them up. Is this not a form of worship?

# CHAPTER 8

# THE SEA! THE SEA!

୬/ଡ

W HEN I WAS first falling for Greece, Ed String-
ham gave me the names of three writers: Lawrence
Durrell, Henry Miller, and Patrick Leigh Fermor. I devoured
Durrell's three lyrical books in order—*Prospero's Cell*, about
Corfu; *Reflections on a Marine Venus*, about Rhodes; and
*Bitter Lemons*, about Cyprus—and was able to introduce Ed
to Gerald Durrell, Lawrence's younger brother, who wrote a
charming memoir, *My Family and Other Animals*, about his
boyhood as a budding naturalist on Corfu. (To Dorothy
Gregory, the famous writing Durrells of Corfu were Larry and
Gerry.) Miller's *Colossus of Maroussi*, about a visit to Greece in
1939 at the invitation of Lawrence Durrell, is a masterpiece,
inimitable, capturing Greece just before the Second World
War. But it was Patrick Leigh Fermor, a British writer and

war hero, who would be my ideal traveling companion. Leigh Fermor—part Pausanias, part Bruce Chatwin—was curious about everything, charismatic, knowledgeable, and inexhaustible. In him I felt I had found a friend.

Leigh Fermor's first claim to fame was as a soldier with the British Army on Crete during the Second World War, when he and a group of Cretan guerrillas kidnapped General Kreipe, the German who commanded the Nazi forces on the island, an exploit that inspired the 1957 movie *Ill Met by Moonlight*. (It was based on a 1950 book by William Stanley Moss, one of the kidnapping crew, and starred Dirk Bogarde as Leigh Fermor, who did not think much of either the book or the film.) Leigh Fermor's writing is dense, fueled by memory, with the breadth of a polymath and the immediacy of personal correspondence. One can picture him crouching in the landscape, jotting notes that will later swell into paragraphs and burgeon into books, with the kind of running heads that are so enticing in the works of a certain British travel-writing genre: "Threshing and Winnowing," "Wine-Dark Words," "Transistrian Cats." He is given to Homeric catalogues—three examples are never enough—and his lists don't peter out but crescendo. In the first few pages of *Mani: Travels in the Southern Peloponnese*, under the heading "Ramifications in the Levant," he lists 91 of the "strange communities" in the worldwide Greek diaspora, including "the Slavophones of Northern Macedonia . . . the phalluswielding Bounariots of Tyrnavos . . . the Venetian nobles of the

Ionian . . . the anchorites of Mt. Athos . . . the cotton-brokers of Alexandria . . . the Greeks of the Danube Delta . . . the Byzantines of Mistra . . . the lunatics of Cephalonia . . . [and] the Hello-boys back from the States." Under "Mosaic Fauna" he describes a Greco-Roman mosaic floor in Sparta—Orpheus, Achilles, Europa—the sole surviving proof of a classical heritage in the modern town, whose warrior ancestors, you may remember, won the Peloponnesian War but evidently lost the race for enduring monuments.

Leigh Fermor is a cult figure among philhellenes, especially among the British, and was exceptionally well connected in Greece. With his wife, Joan, a photographer, whom he met in Cairo in the forties, he settled in Kardamyli (Karda*meli*), a remote town on the western coast of the Mani. There he wrote his best-known book, *A Time of Gifts* (1977), about his journey as a young man, in the early thirties, from the Hook of Holland to Constantinople, on foot. The journey was continued in *Between the Woods and the Water* (1986) and *The Broken Road* (2013), which was published posthumously (it ends in midsentence; one hates to say it, but he did die, in 2011). Leigh Fermor viewed his youthful adventures as if through the wrong end of a telescope: distant yet detailed, like an exquisite miniature.

There is something contagious about the writing of Patrick Leigh Fermor. It makes people want to follow in his footsteps. A young writer named Nick Hunt walked 2,500 miles through Europe, retracing Leigh Fermor's route for *Walking the Woods and the Water* (2014). More recently, a Dutch artist and birder named Jacques Grégoire has produced a series of watercolors from the same European walking tour for a project called From the North Sea to the Black Sea. I followed in Leigh Fermor's footsteps, albeit by car, in 2000, driving the coastal route around the Mani peninsula, from Kalamata to Cape Tenaro, the entrance to Hades, and back. The house he built, with Joan, in Kardamyli, a storied town about a quarter of the way down the western coast of the Mani, loomed large in my imagination, especially after I found out that the Leigh Fermors had left their house to the Benaki Museum, which hoped to turn it into a center for international literary events and a residence for writers.

I had learned from an item in the *Times Literary Supplement* that one could book a tour of the house in Kardamyli for ten euros—and the cost of getting there, of course. So the next time I was in Greece, in March of 2017, fulfilling a long-held dream of returning to the Aegean to stay longer than I did the first time, thirty years earlier, I wrote a careful letter, in Greek, to the Benaki, vetted by my latest Greek teacher, Chrysanthe, requesting permission to visit the Kardamyli house. I found it difficult to read the reply, partly because it was written in bureaucratic Greek and partly because I didn't like what it said. Apparently the museum was awaiting work permits, and as soon as those permits came through, the house would be closed to visitors so that restoration work, paid for by the

Stavros Niarchos Foundation, could begin. I would just miss the chance, unless . . . Well, this was Greece, after all, and it was possible that the permits would be delayed. I decided to trust the Greek gods, add Kardamyli to my itinerary, and hope for the best.

KARDAMYLI IS MENTIONED by Homer in the *Iliad*: Agamemnon promises the region to Achilles if he will rejoin the battle against Troy. (You may remember that Achilles spends most of the *Iliad* sulking in his tent and is drawn back to battle only to avenge his friend Patroclus, who, having disguised himself in Achilles' armor to put fear into the Trojans, is slain by Hector.) The town is exceptionally well sited: it's protected from severe weather to the east by Mount Taygetus, the gigantic mountain of the Peloponnese that slopes all the way to the tip of the Mani; to the west, it looks out over the Messenian Gulf to the westernmost peninsula of the southern Peloponnese. Winds from the west keep Kardamyli temperate even in winter. Although Achilles refused all Agamemnon's gifts, he did rejoin the war, and after his death it is said that his son Neoptolemus came to collect.

Leigh Fermor never worried that Kardamyli would become a tourist destination, because it is so remote. Neoptolemus probably arrived by boat. The trip overland has been made easier in recent years by a modern highway from Corinth to Kalamata, at the base of the peninsula. But it takes an intrepid driver to negotiate the tortuous drive from Kalamata over and down to Kardamyli. On the map the road loops back and forth like a diagram of the small intestine. But it is in the large intestine that one feels the twists and turns of the mountain road, negotiating the switchbacks and running along high precipices; one moment the sea is far down on your right, and then suddenly, dizzyingly, it's on your left. It reminded me of a bus ride I took on the island of Ithaca, which twists in the middle like a Möbius strip. After about thirty kilometers, Kardamyli comes into view, down at sea level. At the bottom of the road, you can make a sharp right to the town beach, with a strip of hotels and restaurants, or stay to the left and drive through the center: two rival grocery stores right next to each other, a fishing dock down on the water, restaurants with terraces overlooking the sea, cafés along the main street, a newsstand, a shop or two specializing in olive oil, and a hardware store with a faded sign that advertises paint in bright colors—*chrómata*. Just outside town to the south is the Kalamitsi Hotel, a palatial establishment, built of the local stone, with arched windows and a red-tiled roof. Leigh Fermor had once written that there was no better place to write than a hotel room in Kardamyli, so while I was waiting and hoping to visit his house I stayed in a room here with a balcony and a spectacular view out over a grove of well-tended olive and citrus trees to the sea.

I could hear the sea, and also the fluting of doves, an insistent three-note figure that would have driven me crazy if I didn't try to tame it by hearing it as syllables of English. It sounded like "Your Birth Day!" or "Your Broom Stick!" One melodious song I traced to a black bird with an orange beak perched in a lemon tree. Sheep bleated, and there was the tinkle of goat bells. There was also, right below me one day, bluegrass music. Kardamyli that week was host to an international jazz festival, and the hotel was full of German, Norwegian, and American musicians.

The hotel had a steep stone stairway down to a private beach. I trotted down there right away. A couple were sunning themselves and ignored me. A white-haired man with one eye squinched shut debouched from the staircase to take a swim, and I automatically started to leave. "You don't have to go—you can stay," he said, in accented English. I explained that I didn't have my bathing suit, which was true. It is also true that I like having a beach to myself.

Once back in my room, it was hard to leave and impossible to stop looking. The sun left a pink smear above the distant gray-blue peninsula, and the sea was like a bolt of ice-blue satin, with matching sky, except that the colors of the air were not as nuanced, having no surface, existing as pure distance measured in light. In the grove in the foreground the trunks of the olive trees twisted seductively. A tongue of sea eased in from the Messenian Gulf below a steep hillside covered with pines, plane trees, and pointed cypresses. Below them, the water was an especially hypnotic shade of deep gray-green-blue, perhaps reflecting the jade green of the trees. Mount Taygetus rose above, catching the light of the setting sun: gray and craggy with scarps of yellow-orange rock and swaths and patches of livid green. As when someone who knows how rich she is, how sufficient her home and income, views the homes and possessions of others without a pinch of envy, so I enjoyed my view of the sea from this stony perch in the hotel. I was looking at the depths of color on the surface—isn't that where the radical beauty lurks? The only thing lacking was a seventh sense to take it in with. When you're traveling, you have a heightened sense of things, and what I was feeling was a kind of historical-hysterical envelopment by beauty.

I pried myself away to cultivate the newsstand, which had a handmade signboard out front that read "Εφημερίδες, βιβλία!" "Newspapers, books!" (The Greek for newspapers is related to the English "ephemera": things that last but a day.) The store also advertised hiking maps and "Handmade affairs." The owner, behind the counter, was grizzled and handsome, barely tolerant toward the Germans who had come in before me, but willing to sell them his handmade affairs. An old Maniot came in, a regular, and the owner automatically reached under the counter and slapped down the customer's favorite newspaper. The old man pointed to the headline and groaned as he opened his coin purse: another round of cuts to pensions had been announced—yet a deeper reach into the Greeks' pockets to pay the country's debts and keep it in the Eurozone. How bitter for the Greeks to be punished like this, to have their circumstances straitened in their old age.

The shop had a display unit for pens and pencils in the form of a giant novelty pencil tip, like a sharpened torpedo, from the famous German pencil maker Staedtler. I wanted a picture of it but knew better than to whip out my cell phone and start framing a shot. I browsed the pencils and racked my brain for the Greek idiom for "take a picture." Finally, I approached the counter and asked the owner, literally, "Please, can I pull a photo of your big lead?" It sounded obscene, but he did not overreact. He nodded ναι, narrowing his eyes and bringing his palms close together to indicate that I should focus strictly on the big pencil. "I don't want to show everything," he said.

I could not have chosen a person less likely to cooperate when I attempted to draw out this Maniot newsagent. I asked which newspaper was the favorite of the older customers in town, and he refused to say. "I read a lot of newspapers," he said. "My opinions I reserve for my family." This turns out to be a typical Maniot response. If you ask someone in Kardamyli to recommend a restaurant, he will demur, pointing out that, on the one hand, a person might like this restaurant, and, on the other hand, another person might like that restaurant. And then he'll turn the question around and ask which restaurants *you* like.

I wanted to give the store my business. It stocked books by Patrick Leigh Fermor—I loved seeing his name in Greek: Πάτρικ

Λη Φέρμορ—but I didn't want to try to read him in translation, and I already owned all his books except *A Time to Keep Silence*, about staying in monasteries, which the store didn't carry. There were some new volumes of letters—Leigh Fermor was a prodigious letter writer—but they were too heavy to carry back to the States, as was the biography, *Patrick Leigh Fermor: An Adventure*, by Artemis Cooper. But there was a slim volume, from a small press, called *Drink Time!*, by Dolores Payás, Leigh Fermor's Spanish translator, who had visited him at his house in Kardamyli in his final years, and I bought that.

As I was leaving, the owner asked where I was from and what I did for work. I told him I was a writer from New York. He chose a Plato bookmark for me and said, "I hope you write many books." That was as close as I got to a blessing on my literary enterprise in Greece.

I SPENT MORE TIME on my balcony, looking at the sea, than I did hiking or swimming or driving around in the Mani. I had finally matured into the kind of traveler who can stay in one place and soak it up. Reading the book by Dolores Payás on my balcony, I was pleased to learn that my view was the same one that Patrick and Joan Leigh Fermor had fallen in love with years ago: deep-green cypresses and soft-green pines descending a steep hill to the beach, with a border of olive and citrus trees. They had camped out on their land while designing and building their house, which took three years. Leigh Fermor went swimming every day, making his way down to the beach by rough stairs cut into the stone, like the ones at the hotel. He stashed walking sticks at strategic points along the way. Dolores Payás wrote that he left the doors and windows open all the time—once, a goat ran through the house. I thought this might be the local custom: the door to the balcony was open when I was let into the hotel room, and my instinct was to leave it like that. Why would you shut out the light, the air, that view for even an instant?

The Leigh Fermors were not initially welcomed by the locals. When they built a hut on the beach, it was dynamited. The town mayor got the locals to accept the British couple by putting out word that Patrick Leigh Fermor was a hero of the Resistance in Crete, having masterminded the kidnapping of General Kreipe. The mayor also sent his daughter Elpida to keep house for them. Joan died at the house in Kardamyli in 2003. She loved cats, and there was a cat door in the master bedroom. On the day she died, several Greek cats were keeping her company. Leigh Fermor became nearly blind with age—he wore an eyepatch and glasses—but he could always keep track of his wineglass.

Along the horizon stretched the peninsula of Messenia, with sandy Pylos, home of honey-voiced Nestor, on the far side, facing west. Nestor is the old man of the *Iliad*, the lord of the Western approaches (in Fitzgerald's phrase): he ruled the Ionian Sea. Modern history has overtaken Pylos, which is now celebrated as the site of a decisive battle in the Greek War of Independence—the Battle of Navarino, in 1827—in which the Turks and Egyptians were defeated at sea by an alliance of British, French, and Russian forces. Nestor would have had a bird's-eye view of the conflict from his palace on the headland and would no doubt have had something to say about it. His best fighting days over, he went to Troy as a counselor to the Achaeans. Every time Homer gives Nestor the floor, the action stalls while the old guy gasses away. In his prime a "master charioteer," he holds up a chariot race during the funeral games for Patroclus to advise his son to hold tight in the turns. In a telling touch, he brought his own gold wine cup to Troy. Nestor's cup is famous, both for its description in the *Iliad* and in the annals of epigraphy: a piece of pottery found on Ischia, near Naples, bears an inscription that, in one of the earliest known uses of the Greek alphabet (circa 740 BC), identifies it as Nestor's cup. At first it seems as if packing along a cup is just a crotchet of old age, but what makes you feel more at home than drinking from your own cup? Nestor was bringing sandy Pylos with him to Troy.

Nestor is one of the lucky ones whose voyage home from Troy was without incident. The Nestoriad would be a snooze. Perhaps his role in the *Iliad* is to give the Achaeans something stable against which to measure their own experience. All the Achaeans long for home, of course; the hope of any soldier going off to war is that he will return home. Nestor's is the supreme example of a successful homecoming. His very name suggests it: *nóstos*, homecoming, from the verb *néomai*, to return home. The word nostalgia yokes the notion of homecoming to the Greek for pain: homesickness. The longing for home is what drives Odysseus.

Long-winded Nestor is pivotal to the *Odyssey* as well. On the advice of Mentor (Athena), Telemachus sets off for sandy Pylos to ask the old king if he knows what happened to his father, Odysseus. "While Nestor talked, the sun went down the sky / and gloom came on the land." In other words, everyone started to yawn. On Nestor's advice, Telemachus travels overland to Sparta, where he meets Menelaus and Helen, but he does not stay long, telling the king, "Longing has come upon me to go home." On his return to Pylos, he asks his companion, Nestor's son Peisistratus, to please drop him off at the ship, because the old king will no doubt bid him a long goodbye, pack a lunch, offer gifts, and delay his departure.

By this time, I was feeling a bit nostalgic myself. I had been away from home for three months, and was replete with beauty. I'd spent a month on Rhodes, one of the sunniest places in the Mediterranean, where I'd picked ambrosial oranges in a grove belonging to my teacher's family, and another month on Patmos, where, on Holy Thursday at the monastery of St. John the Theologian, I bore witness as the Holy Spirit hovered over the washing of the feet in the form of a drone. I'd spent three nights on cosmopolitan Mykonos, and three days exploring neighboring Delos, the uninhabited island and open-air museum, sacred to Apollo. And I had come from the Aegean to the Ionian, to the very birthplace of nostalgia, to visit the home of a writer whom, I suddenly realized, I thought of as my literary father.

Nostalgia may mean a yearning for a place, but it is also a yearning for a time when you were in that place and therefore for the you of the past. Revisiting the Aegean had given me more than a few Wordsworthian moments as I strove to reconcile myself now, sitting on a balcony enjoying the view, with that earlier self, hopping from ferry to ferry, trying to plumb the depths of the wine-dark sea and master a language that a better linguist than I could founder in. I had struggled and struggled in Greek, only to realize that my modern Greek had peaked early, on my second trip, in 1985, when, on the island of Kefalonia, in the Ionian Sea, I tried on a two-piece bathing suit and, emerging from the fitting room, said spontaneously to the salesgirl, "Είμαι παχιά"—"I'm fat"—nailing the feminine ending on a difficult class of Greek adjective. The salesgirl gave me a drawn-out "Οοοχι!"—"Noooooo!"—and made the sale. I got ripples of sunburn on my virgin midriff.

I knew a lot of Greek, but I wouldn't say I spoke modern Greek or call myself a classicist, either. I was more in love with the language than it was with me. My mind was like a riverbed that had silted up: it had its own archaeological strata from which an occasional find emerged. I had not mastered the language, ancient or modern, but I got glimpses of its genius, its patterns, the way it husbanded the alphabet, stretching those twenty-four letters to record everything anyone could ever want to say.

For all I knew, this would be my last trip to Greece—it was undeniably the last to date, and the longest. I once harbored a desire to spend an entire year here, from solstice to solstice and equinox to equinox, and back to solstice again. Now I wondered if that wouldn't feel like exile. I had something in common with Patrick Leigh Fermor: I had a history in Greece, memories of youthful travels, and could compose my own catalogue in the style of the master: watching the mummified body of St. Spyridon being carried through the streets of Corfu Town, swaying jauntily in his upright glass coffin, on Palm Sunday ("There is nothing more picturesque than Corfu at Easter," Dorothy Gregory had written to me); taking a wrong turn on Naxos with my friend Paula and accidentally touring emery-mining country (who knew?), marveling at the system of antique chair lifts for hauling the mineral out of the gorge, and skidding onto the white pebble beach of Lionas at the end of the road, with its crystalline water beckoning and the locals coming out to wave hello; waking in a bare-bones hotel room in the mountains of Cyprus to the sound of Greek men twittering like birds in the *kafeneíon* across the street; speeding through the landscape of Antiparos with Cynthia, my fellow-philhellene, at the wheel, huntresses in pursuit of the perfect taverna; laughing with Andreas the Turk on a bus that was stuck in traffic in Athens as he explained why he didn't like Starbucks ("They don't have Nescafé"). There were still places I wanted to go—Sifnos, Kythera, Poros, Folegandros, Nisyros, Spetses, Hydra—and I would never stop trying to master the language. But I found I could say with Telemachus that longing had come upon me to go home.

AT LAST THE DAY CAME when I got the OK: I could visit the house of Patrick Leigh Fermor. I had written again to the Benaki (in English this time) and heard back that the permits had in fact been delayed. The house had been emptied of books and furniture, but the work had not yet begun, and, owing to popular demand, the Benaki was permitting tours. I dressed carefully: a sun hat instead of a baseball cap, a stiff underwire bra instead of a sports bra—I felt like I was hoisting a breastplate worthy of Athena—my best-fitting black pants, a blue top with a turquoise shirt over it, and hiking boots instead of sandals. I carried only a small shoulder bag with my sunglasses, phone, notebook, and wallet. Nothing extra—no sunscreen or beach gear. This was a serious, single-minded mission. I took a shortcut through the olive grove. Yellow butterflies fluttered in the trees, as if sharing my excitement—the pathetic fallacy! The path was littered with what I at first took for animal droppings, but as I passed a ewe nosing aside her nursing lamb, I realized that I was under a mulberry tree in full fruit. I sampled the mulberries and gathered some in my hat to offer as a gift to the housekeeper, Mrs. Elpida Beloyianni, who I knew by now was the same Elpida who had worked for Leigh Fermor, depicted in Dolores Payás's book. The Benaki had kept her on as caretaker.

A German couple was there when I arrived. Then a chatty English couple I recognized from breakfast at the hotel drove up. There was a gray car parked outside, with flat tires and a peeling roof. We would learn that it was Leigh Fermor's car, kept for his guests' convenience. The wall around the house had double doors, painted blue, with small high grilled windows, which a tall person could peer through. The shade of blue was one I saw often in the Mani: a perfect blend of pale blue, pale green, and pale gray—glaucous! Often while traveling in Greece I had stood outside a closed door and felt frustrated: if you can't open a door, it might as well not exist. But a door that opens, as this one now did, framing Elpida, is an invitation to a whole world that had previously been denied. Elpida had red hair with gray roots and was wearing an oversized black T-shirt with three sets of big smooching lips on it in turquoise, peach, and royal blue.

Inside, we were still outside. We entered an arched stone passageway, paved with pebble mosaics and open to the sky. "Ghika designed the mosaic," Elpida said, gesturing, in English. ("Who is Ghika?" the British woman asked me. "A painter," I said, feeling superior. Nikos Ghika and his wife, Tiggie, short for Antigone, were friends of the Leigh Fermors. Ghika had given his house in Athens to the Benaki. It is now a studio museum.) There was art by Ghika built into the walls as well: a stone face sculpted into a plaster wall surrounded by a dotted red line, with the word ΠΡΟΣΟΧΗ!—CAUTION!—hand-lettered under it. Within what might have been a window frame was a chalky stippled painting in pale blues and browns, of a cat (or maybe a fox) standing on its hind legs to reach a fish. Houses in Kardamyli—all over the Mani, in fact—are built from the native stone, quarried out of Mount Taygetus. I had seen men along the road chipping stones into rough blocks with mallet and chisel. There is something so autochthonous about the way Europeans build their homes from the local stone—the stone cottages of the Cotswolds, the yellow sandstone of Sicily, the black lava of Catania—quarrying it out of the mountains and taming it into blocks, turning the earth inside out and stitching it up in walls on the other side. In the Mani, builders make jokes in the stone and plant self-portraits in the walls. Leigh Fermor had shells embedded in the rocks surrounding one window. A narrow vertical niche alongside a door had glass shelves in it and a mirror behind them that reflected whoever was trying to peer inside. Doors along an arcade led to bedrooms, the kitchen, and a staircase to a lower level. Elpida opened the door to the master bedroom, which I knew from the Payás book had been Joan's room: someone had placed a small mirror near the bottom to block the cat door. Leigh Fermor slept in his studio in a separate building.

The living and dining room was huge, with a bay of windows at one end and low, built-in platforms along it, padded with thin mattresses, as if for a symposium. Rickety book-shelves rose along all the walls. The books had been removed to the Benaki for restoration. The fireplace was in the shape of a flame, modeled after an architectural flourish from a mosque in Istanbul. "He was a traveler," Elpida said, explaining the own-er's taste. The ceiling was coffered wood and the floor was stone. In the center of the room was a slab of porphyry shaped like a many-pointed star. "We'll take it," one of the Germans joked.

Why had I wanted to come here? What did I expect to see? How did I expect this house to bring me closer to Patrick Leigh Fermor, the philhellenes' philhellene? Leigh Fermor was very sociable—he had chosen Kardamyli over Crete because it was more isolated and if he lived in Crete he'd never get any work done. I was glad the place was unfurnished, though I would have loved to see the books. I asked Elpida where the drinks table had stood. Dolores Payás had described it, and the endless supply of wine, Nemean red. Maybe that's why I liked this place, this house, this headland of the Peloponnese: it had that quality of Greece I most admired—it was spare and giving at the same time.

In the garden, paved with stones and pebble mosaics, there were beds of rosemary, overgrown, and wooden benches circling olive trees. Stone benches enclosed the far end, over the drop to the sea, framed to the left by the same stand of pine and cypress that I could see from my hotel balcony. I knew that out here somewhere were the stairs to the beach.

Back inside, Elpida waited patiently. The British couple,

who were from Bath, asked if this was a good time to pay. It was five euros apiece, Elpida said, but I had only a ten-euro note, and she didn't have change. I said I would happily donate the extra five euros, but she complained, "Then I will have to write another receipt!" and gave me the change out of her own pocket. I hung around for as long as I could, offering her the mulberries (she took one out of politeness). "Είναι δύσκολο να φύγει," I said, getting the person wrong ("It is difficult for *him* to leave" instead of "It is difficult for *me* to leave"). She let it pass.

I WENT TO the Kalamitsi town beach afterward, down the road from Leigh Fermor's house. It was hard walking—the stones were the size of fists. I crunched along toward some big rocks in the direction of my hotel. I wasn't sure I could get past them, but I always have to see what is around the bend, and I still wanted to find the stone stairs leading to Leigh Fermor's beach. So I picked my way around the rocks, and beyond them was a secluded cove with three cypress trees and gigantic, impassable rocks on the other side. There, camouflaged by lichen, was a narrow stone flight of stairs cut into the cliff, with a padlocked gate at the third step. These were Leigh Fermor's stairs, and I was on the beach from which he swam every day.

I parked myself on a comfortable rock and looked at the view: rocks, sea, cypresses, an offshore island. The yellow butterflies were down here on the beach, too. I wanted to go for a swim and thought of my Speedo hanging from the clothesline on the hotel balcony. I could swim in my underwear, but that would make for an uncomfortable walk home. I decided to risk it. Yes, Reader, I stripped again—shirt, boots, pants, bra, and underwear—and picked my way over the stones until I could flop facedown in the water. It was exhilarating to paddle around in this sparkling place! There was a riffle on the surface a ways out, where there must have been a reef, but it was easy to imagine that the water had been kicked up by a chorus line of nymphs. All the movement in the water seemed animated, intentional, fueled by personality—some god or monster might rise from it any second. I swam around one of the big rocks and discovered a cave, where the water made weird sucking sounds. I did not investigate. Hearing the tinkle of bells, I spotted some goats jumping from high rocks down to the shore. This made me glad—I'd never seen goats from out in the water before. I swam back to the beach and clambered over the wet stones to my rock, where I air-dried in the breeze. The swim had relaxed me and I had lost all fear that anyone would come trekking over those treacherous rocks, so I was astonished to look up and see a young man with dark hair and a backpack and hiking boots approaching from the way I had come. I screamed and grabbed my shirt to cover my front. "Excuse me!" I yelled. "I thought I had complete privacy!" He made a motion that it was OK, breasts are fine, no need to cover up. He walked past and then took off his own clothes and waded into the water, where he splashed around a bit but did not immerse himself. I was trying not to stare, or at least not to be caught staring, but I watched out of the corner of my eye as he got out of the water, took a sketchbook out of his pack, and, crouching there on the beach, drew in it or wrote for a while.

I pulled on my pants and shirt at about the same time the young man did, stuffing my underwear in my hat. I nodded goodbye, fully clothed, as he left, circling behind me, and followed him out shortly after. I had been caught naked on the beach, one of the most embarrassing things that can happen to a person, short of subsequently having your clothes stolen and having to return home nude, skulking from olive tree to olive tree, as in a dream, hoping a shepherd will come by and lend you a fleece. I thought of the myths of mortals stumbling onto Artemis or Aphrodite bathing in the woods. The only nude art I resembled was a portrait by Lucian Freud. But nothing terrible had happened—my encounter left no residue of guilt or shame. Nobody cared that I sat naked on a beach in the Peloponnese. On Patrick Leigh Fermor's beach I was allowed.

On the way back to the hotel, I kept feeling a vibration coming from the hat—which was in my hand, not on my head—and I thought it was my cell phone. But my phone was in my shoulder bag with my notebook and wallet and glasses. Before going into my room at the hotel, I set the hat upside down on a low stone wall, and as I pulled out my intimates a yellow butterfly shot into the garden.

# Acknowledgments

As THE ROSY FINGERS of dawn touch the tops of the buildings that pass for the Acropolis in my neighborhood, I wish to express my gratitude to all earlier writers, travelers, scholars, translators, and philhellenes—behind every word of mine they stand in their legions, nearly three thousand years' worth of language and scholarship.

Fleets of people brought this book home. Foremost among them is Matt Weiland, my editor at W. W. Norton, who surprised and delighted me by suggesting that I write about Greece and then patiently gave form to chaos, and even learned a word of Greek (ο ράφτης!).

Next comes David Kuhn, of Aevitas Creative Management, and with him Nate Muscato and Becky Sweren, who shared the excitement of creating something new out of something ancient.

Assistance arrived from all over. From Corfu came Dorothy Gregory, a teacher who gave constant encouragement and who lives on in the memory of everyone whose life she touched. Chrysanthe Filippardos, another generous teacher, welcomed me to her home in Astoria and sent me to her village in Rhodes. Kostas Christoforatos, of Kefalonia, made friendly corrections to my stumbling Greek. Peter Bien counselled me on Greek and Greeklish from his mountain home in the Adirondacks. Cynthia Cotts shared her expertise in modern Greek, along with the occasional bottle of assyrtiko.

Froma Zeitlin, of Princeton University, emerged from the past. Laura M. Slatkin and Charles Mercier came to my rescue with their abundant stores of knowledge. On the coast of Maine, Caroline Alexander did triple duty as classicist, writer, and host.

The fact checker Bobby Baird and the copy editor Elizabeth Macklin kept me from coming to grief. John McPhee offered notes on the geology of Cyprus and the Acropolis. John Bennet, Nicolas Niarchos, and Bruce Diones expressed enthusiasm at critical moments. Nick Trautwein and Dorothy Wickenden dropped names I lunged for. Gifts from Edward M. Stringham kept giving from my bookshelves. And, lest we forget, *The New Yorker* and Advance Publications underwrote my Greek studies for years. I hope they do not regret it.

On Rhodes, I was befriended by Eleni Skourtou and Vasilia Kazoulli, of the University of the Aegean. In Athens, Eugenia Tzirtzilaki and George Kolyvas heartened me, as did Richard Moore. Friends who have given me their companionship in

Greece include Nancy Holyoke, Dwight Allen, Karl Rohr, Denise Rodino, Sam Rodino, the late Bill Gifford, Gregory Maguire, Hylary Kingham, Paula Rothstein, Cynthia Cotts (again!), and Angelika Gräwer (a.k.a. Anna of Patmos). Kevin Conley opened the way for travel in 2012 with Deborah Ziska, Cristy Meiners, James Conaway, Andreas Stamatiou, and Andreas Spyrou, a trip that led to a correspondence with Mrs. Myrto Kaouki, of the Benaki Museum, and, ultimately, the road to Kardamyli.

Inspiration came from Nashville in the form of F. Lynne Bachleda, Annie Freeman, Alan LeQuire, and Wesley Paine. Thanks to a residency with the Victoria Literary Festival on Prince Edward Island, I parleyed with Pam Price, Linda Gilbert, Emma Price, J. C. Humphreys, Mo Duffy Cobb, and Lexie and Leah Wood, who helped me reinvent the Greek alphabet. Peter Sokolowski is my man at Merriam-Webster. Andrea Roccella passed along the lore of his native Sicily; John Pope weighed in from New Orleans on Phi Beta Kappa; from Skyros and Amsterdam came books and clippings from Jaco de Groot. Back home in New York, I got a boost from Linda Angrilli, of FIT, and I found kindred spirits in Ann Patty, a late-blooming Latinist; Cindy Calder, an educator and lifelong philhellene; and Susanna Coffey, a keeper of the flame. George Gibson put me in touch with Nicholas Humez; Noreen Tomassi introduced me to Elaine Moore Hirsch; Walter Strachowsky left serendipitous books at my door; Jane Schramm sent them in the mail. And I will never forget my work with Eslee Samberg.

ACKNOWLEDGMENTS

W. W. Norton, my publisher, has showered me with blessings. Special thanks to Julia Reidhead, Nancy Palmquist, Don Rifkin, Ingsu Liu, Anna Oler, Erin Sinesky Lovett, Dan Christiaens, Zarina Patwa, and Remy Cawley, as well as to Nick Misani for the dazzling cover.

The Tahoe Girls—Mary Grimm, Susan Grimm, Tricia Springstubb, and Kristin Olson—draw me ever upward with their perceptive readings and brilliant critiques. The Kelleys Island crew—Charles Oberndorff, Jeff Gundy, Donna Jarrell, Susan Carpenter, Laura Walter, and Jackie Cummins—give me an anchor in my natal waters of Lake Erie.

For their sustaining friendships, I thank Denise Rodino, Clancey O'Connor, Ann Goldstein, Elizabeth Pearson-Griffiths, Toby Allan Schust, Emily Nunn, Dan Kaufman, Sharon Cameron, Barrett Mandel, Alice Truax, Janet Abramowicz, Vicki Desjardins, Ladi Dell'aira, Penelope Rowlands, J. Kathleen White, Penny Lynn White, Vicky Raab, Nancy Woodruff Hamilton, and the ghost of Lindsley Cameron Miyoshi.

It was my brother Miles who appointed himself my original writing teacher and who first interpreted a word of Greek for me ("Eureka!" "You stink!") at the Lyceum. It is my sister Dee who keeps me honest and fires me up.